TIMELESS Vol. I

FIVE
FUNDAMENTAL
BUSINESS DESIGN
PRINCIPLES

*A new model to craft successful
design-driven businesses,
brands & strategies*

GIANLUCA CINQUEPALMI

FOREWORD

There are several reasons why I decided to write this book. The main one was to satisfy my curiosity about the true meaning of business design. To look beyond the obvious and not just accept things the way they are, to investigate what's out there and why. Over the years I have collected meaningful thoughts and best practices about design, branding and business. There is a ton of knowledge available at our fingertips, but it is surprising how little of it we actually grasp.

Timeless was born from the desire to share a different point of view, to illustrate a road map and trigger the thinking process towards the creation of valuable, sustainable and innovative design businesses.

Why Timeless? One of my life undertaking is the reflection and fascination in creating design that can be defined as "Timeless", products and objects that become better with use, or those that possess an essential, effortless elegance. Experiences that remain remarkable, no matter our age or status. Likewise trying to challenge how our world moves and behaves nowadays, in a constant rush, with almost everything being made disposable, and with very little thought about the future impact of our actions.

This book will guide you through my journey in creating an unconventional framework to asses and develop valuable, sustainable and innovative brands, designs and businesses. This very framework has been my guiding principle throughout the last few years of design practice, and I hope we can begin to build a different perspective towards design and business.

Early in my career, one of the dynamics that fascinated me the most was the volatility of status of certain products, services and institutions, going from hero to zero in the blink of an eye.

We live in a complicated world. It is hyper-dynamic, hyper-connected and hyper-competitive. A simple explanation of such dynamics was not plausible. So I began researching patterns and theories that would help me decode such behaviours.

Throughout my research I discovered five main attributes that most successful design businesses share. Surprisingly enough, they go beyond simple form or function.

Why five? Well, the number five seems to be a constant in my life, from my date of birth to my last name "Cinquepalmi", which contains the Italian word for five: "Cinque". Aside from this, fivefold conceptual schemes have been used for millennia to aid understanding and memorisation of complex phenomena: alchemy, interaction of the natural elements, geomancy, Feng Shui, astrology, music, military strategy and martial arts are just some examples *(plus we also have five fingers, making it easy to keep count)*. So why not learn from the past to improve the future?

I often encounter companies and institutions that have a very cynical approach towards design and business, using design only as a means of generating profit rather than innovation. To me, design is never cynical or arbitrary, and seeing it as such, denies an essential aspect of business; its social and cultural value. We should never forget that companies are social institutions just as much as financial ones.

I believe we *(entrepreneurs, design professionals, creative minds)* should strive to infuse deep cultural and social value into our work. When crafting something, we must inspire people who interact with our work to know and feel that they are not just buying another piece of merchandise. Instead, they should perceive the acquisition of new knowledge, a fragment of culture. At the end of the day, we are not just creating beautiful and useful objects, but also the culture around them.

CONTENTS

to Betta

DEDICATED TO

CULTURE LOVERS

We believe in the beauty of creation,
the intellectual achievements of humanity and the
empowering pursuit of proactively
conserving pieces of great cultural,
social and financial value.

DESIGNERS

We believe that our creations contribute
to the fascinating development of our kind
and we want to leave behind a significant footprint.
We want to create value, while preventing
the demise of something good.

ENTREPRENEURS

We believe in adventure,
and take risks that pay off.
We believe in the sustainable growth
that comes from creating and maintaining
greater values.

THE JOURNEY

Over the past 10 years, I've had the privilege of working both directly and indirectly with some of the most successful brands in the world, and I've learnt something new each time. As I worked on each company's unique selling point and signature style, a few key questions continued to provoke my curiosity:

I. *Is there a common denominator that defines the success or failure of a business?*

II. *What are the key elements that define and distinguish a world-class business from a mundane one?*

III. *Why do some products or services seem to vastly outperform their competition, although both have exactly the same access to talent and technology?*

Why, why, why - I'm obsessed with the why. Why can some designers, businesses, products, services, brands achieve it all and others can't? Why are some companies way up there and then suddenly come crashing down? Why is that? These puzzling questions were well worth investigating.

My investigation started with trying to understand how our economy, or the 'market', has changed. Today, the lines between product design, graphic design, branding, marketing, advertising and business in general are blurring. In our modern society it's inarguable that the general public acknowledges the symbolic value of a product or service more than its functional value. We do not buy another pair of jeans because we need them, but because we want them.

Over the past several decades, we have shifted from an economy focused on industrial production, to one focused around people. Such economy, *(postmodern society)* is not based on rationality. It is based on personal desire, and desire means brand and status.

Most companies now recognise that experiences connected to a product or service are immensely more important than just the look or performance alone.

By analysing my own achievements and my many, many failures while working with a wide range of companies, I decoded five common, fundamental principles:

I.   *Being an absolute innovator does not always pay off, but neither does being a compromised version of someone else. Rather, the most effective way to succeed is to be the best version of ourselves.*

II. *Aesthetics are only one component of the equation. Simply creating beautiful objects or images is no longer enough. Subjectivity, availability and context must always be taken into consideration.*

III. *Brands and businesses need to engage consumers on a deep, intimate level. Talking about bits and bytes, features and benefits is informative and even essential, but it is not sufficient.*

IV. *Consumers are increasingly superficial. They now live in a world with too many choices and too little time, so a rational, investigative process is out of the question. They refer to price, position and buzz to make their buying decisions in the shortest amount of time possible.*

V.   *Finally, any brand must master the fundamental skill of creating and maintaining relationships based on trust, constantly expressing and reinforcing its core values, surprising its consumers and ultimately exceeding their expectations.*

THE SIMPLE, THE COMPLICATED AND THE COMPLEX

At this stage, what I thought was a quest to find the "secret recipe" for success (or even better, the equation for success) started becoming more complicated than anticipated.

Early on, I encountered two key topics that proved enlightening. The first was an interesting distinction between science and art, which Prof. Avinash K. Dixit states in his book, *The Art of Strategy*.

> *"Science and art, by their very nature, differ in that science can be learned in a systematic and logical way, whereas expertise in art has to be acquired by example, experience and practice."*

This sentence struck a chord. Maybe the quest was not to find a secret recipe, but rather to analyse and decode my own work and experiences; to learn from mistakes and successes. I always thought that anyone could learn to duplicate a technique, apply the rules and use the latest fashion to create a neat little design. But *is that really a true creative expression?* This led me to question whether we are really creating an impact or whether we are just being incremental *(i.e. making small, irrelevant changes)*.

When we are there, **at the edge of uncertainty, pushing the boundaries of our own personal knowledge**, only then will we find authentic development and true creative expression.

In order to create a true design culture, deep understanding and mastery of techniques is imperative! This is a long process and oftentimes an uncomfortable one. Example, experience and practice are the tools we must use to create real value.

Most designers and entrepreneurs don't believe undergoing this process is their job. They believe that form and function, and making a profit, are sufficient. That's not very constructive. Instead it's just—as previously mentioned—incremental.

The second topic, from the subject of the **science of complexity,** is a revealing classification of problems. In *Getting to Maybe: How the World Is Changed*, Frances Westley, Brenda Zimmerman and Michael Patton propose that there are **three types of problems in the world:**

- **Simple problems**, *such as baking a cake*
- **Complicated problems**, *such as sending a rocket to the moon and*
- **Complex ones,** *like raising a child*

This is a fascinating theory and, astonishingly, it closely matches my design philosophy. The science of complexity, just like design, embraces life as it is: *unpredictable*, *emergent*, *evolving* and *adaptable*.

Often, design is approached as a **simple** task, as if it is simply a matter of cutting and pasting several elements from other successful designs. It is approached as if there is a formula: use this type, that image, grid or shape, follow the recipe, sprinkle some fairy dust on client's ideas and the trick is done. Success guaranteed! Unfortunately, this is not the case.

Sometimes, design is approached as a **complicated** task. It is recognised that a higher level of expertise is needed, with good old fashioned background checks and references completed, an appropriate and accurate plan of action created (a brief), sound preliminary research performed, and all the goals and outcomes meticulously executed. With this process, there is a very high chance of success. After all, we have successfully delivered hundreds of designs, right? Yet even in this scenario, things can go terribly wrong.

Seldom, design is approached as a complex task, although this is how it should be. The crushing reality is that there are no secret formulas or hyper-effective plans guaranteeing the success of our design. Some years of work and study under our belt will provide us with knowledge, expertise and practice but there is NO assurance at all that our future design will be a success.

Design should be approached as a complex task. We must take into consideration countless variables that we might not directly control, from subjectivity of the design itself, to pricing, positioning and accessibility. The success or failure of a design and the related business is determined by the appreciation and consideration by the greater public.

Complex systems, such as human beings, stock markets, global organisations, design, branding and businesses, all share behaviours that cannot be explained by their single components. Citing Kurt Koffka:

The whole is other than the sum of the parts.

In complex systems, relationships are fundamental. It is the connections and relationships between all these parts that define how complex systems work.

A NEW-OLD MODEL

By now I had gained sufficient insight to begin forming my own business design model. I knew that there are at least five key principles and a delicate balance to be maintained in building a successful design or business.

I also knew there is no secret formula, and that rather than focusing on single elements of the design process, it is essential to look at the system as a whole. The goal was not only to provide a practical understanding of a subject, but to make the subject accessible, digestible and usable, without making it simplistic.

Therefore, it was time to sift through my five common, fundamental principles (see pg. 11), and synthesise them into distinctive and memorable key words and their meanings.

I.   Character: *To infuse values;*
II. Desire: *To consider subjectivity and availability;*
III. Empathy: *To engage consumers on a deep, intimate level;*
IV. Trust: *To prove and demonstrate values;*
V.   Consistency: *To constantly reinforce the core values.*

Things started falling into place. This fivefold conceptual scheme perfectly represented my business design model. In good designer spirit, why not learn from the past to improve the future?

I began researching historic models and conceptual themes that have been used to express complicated interactions between elements. I started with the ancient Greek philosopher, Plato. In his dialogue titled "Timaeus", Plato theorised that classical elements were made of regular solids (Platonic Solids). Earth was associated with the hexahedron, air with the octahedron, water with the icosahedron, fire with the tetrahedron, and finally, the universe with the dodecahedron. This led to a further milestone in my reasoning.

According to Plato, the elements are not limited by their form or function, but by their abstract characterisation and properties: earth *(solidity, inertia)*; water *(fluidity, cohesion)*; fire *(temperature, energy content)* air *(mobility, expansion,)*. Wonderful!

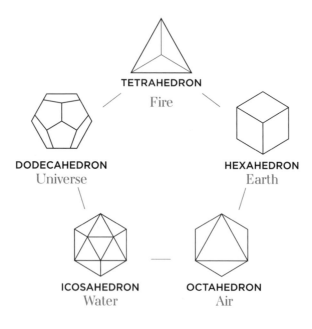

Fig. 1 Temaus

Yet, using this newly gained knowledge, I soon realized a simple listing of five elements was not sufficient to represent the complexity of business design; I needed an **interrelated, interconnected** reference system.

Having lived in Asia for several years, ancient Chinese philosophies were an inevitable and inexhaustible source of inspiration. Many traditional Chinese disciplines use a fivefold conceptual scheme to explain a wide array of phenomena: the concept of Wŭ Xíng (五行). Wŭ Xíng, known as the 'five elements' or 'five phases' has been used for thousands of years as the defining framework for many fields, from traditional Chinese medicine to Feng Shui.

Fascinated by this millenary concept, I pondered whether the same dynamics could apply to business design as well as they applied to so many other fields. While limited by my inability to study directly through the Chinese language, I began researching and comparing similarities between the model I was trying to create and the ancient conceptual scheme of Wŭ Xíng.

This model turned out to be particularly appropriate since the Chinese Wŭ Xíng is primarily concerned with explaining **process** and **change.** Rather than the single elements, what captured my attention were the **interrelated dynamics between them:** the so-called four interweaving cycles.

According to the theory of Wŭ Xíng, the elements/phases are not static entities but rather fluid and dynamic ones.This dynamism is expressed through the four cycles. The Generating (生, shēng) and Controlling (克/剋, kè) cycles represent **balance and harmony in the system**. The other two, the Overacting (cheng) and the Insulting (侮,wŭ), represent imbalance and disharmony.

These cycles and their interaction allow the five elements to function harmoniously. When the five elements are **balanced,** they represent health, prosperity and success. When they're out of balance—overacting, counteracting, or failing to properly support one another—they represent illness, hardship and failure.

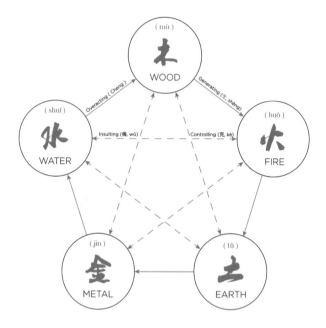

Fig. 2 The Five elements / Phases Wŭ Xíng

Just like in the Chinese Wŭ Xíng, the overall concept here is that in business design we must seek balance between the elements in order for our design to prosper.

In our context, the generating cycle is:

I.   Character feeds Desire *(like wood feeds fire)*

II. Desire feeds Empathy *(like fire feeds earth)*

III. Empathy feeds Trust *(like earth feeds metal)*

IV. Trust feeds consistency *(like metal creates water)*

V.   Consistency feeds Character *(like water feeds wood)*

The overacting and insulting cycles are slightly different. A lack of character impacts empathy and trust, a lack of trust impacts character and desirability, a lack of desirability impacts trust and consistency, a lack of consistency impacts desirability and empathy, and finally, a lack of empathy impacts consistency and character.

Although this may seem esoteric, it actually has more to do with common sense than anything else. The essence here is to realise that multiple factors influence the success or failure of a design, and even more so if we look at business design.

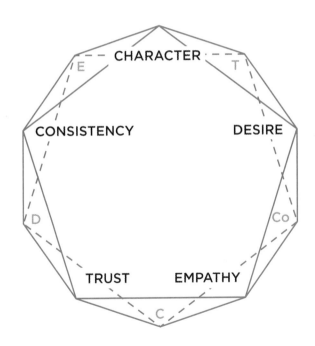

Fig. 3 Timeless Diamond Elements & Interaction

THE SYSTEM AT WORK

After this discovery, I began testing my model both as a developing framework and a method of evaluation in order to verify the viability of it.

Analysing my very own projects (both successful and unsuccessful) and trying to see how my model would or could apply, I started with a spider-graph. The five elements were placed at the vertex, and the evaluated project was ranked from 1 to 5 for each principle, using 1 as the lowest and 5 as the highest score. Finally, I analysed the sequencing of how I had approached each design project.

Unsurprisingly (*not true—very surprisingly!*), the most successful designs I'd produced, the ones that were better perceived and accepted by the public were: 1. the ones that **followed a clear developmental sequence**; and 2. the ones where the **5 principles were more balanced**.

For instance, let's say we had to redesign a jam jar. The correct approach would be to start identifying the **character** *(the core distinctive, unique values)* of the brand: heritage, handmade, all natural, grandma's secret and so on. Then we focus on the **desirable** component of the design *(aesthetics, ergonomics, price and position)*. While developing this design solution we should also focus on the core messages and values that will **empathise** with a specific target: Are we selling to moms or health conscious young adults; is it *"like grandma made it"* or *"nutritious & sugar free"*.

Now, we must make our message credible by demonstrating to our target that they can **trust** our offering. To do so we must be truthful when we say *"like grandma made it"* or *"nutritious & sugar free"*. We must be **consistent** with our promise and reinforce the brand values and narrative: *"If grandma was a vegan, she would have chosen XYZ Brand"*.

On the other hand, the most unsatisfactory designs I had produced didn't have a developmental sequence. Instead, they were merely incremental and unbalanced, with peaks of attention on only one or two elements such as desire *(aesthetics)* and trust *(message)*, and with complete disregard for the others.

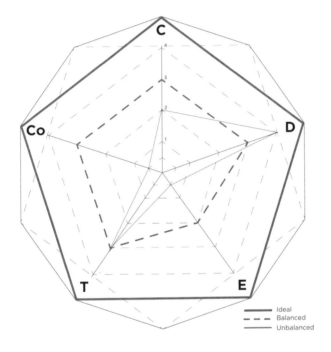

Ideal
Balanced
Unbalanced

For example a marketing manager told me: XYZ Brand is a grandma's jam brand but there is a market in the sugar free and healthy segment, so let's just make a sexy jar that says sugar free. And unfortunately I did.

The model is a tool to address and ease the complexity of design. Its aim is to give you a different perspective on how complex systems such as business design can be approached and successfully implemented. In the following chapters, I will elaborate on each principle one by one, sharing some thinking points on how to better approach each principle.

At the end of the book I will present a simple case study to illustrate how the model can be brought to fruition.

THE FIVE PRINCIPLES

CHARACTER

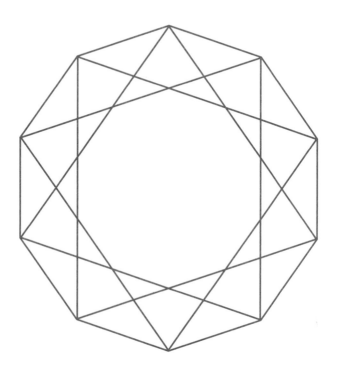

In this context, character is defined as *the distinctive nature of something.*

It is conceptually simple: character is created and maintained by being recognisably different in nature from our competitors, even if we are selling a similar product or service.

Having character means being able to synthesise and communicate the key differentiating factors that make us stand apart from the crowd. Character is rooted in the ability to understand and express our current position as well as our desired future direction.

The public must be made to feel a specific emotion that will immediately and clearly represent what our product or service stands for.

Ultimately, developing character means shifting our vision from **what we do** to **the value we provide.**

Inspiration:

Character can be associated with the Chinese element wood 木, as in nature we will never find a single plant that is identical to another.

Wood represents 'Qi' and is the symbol of: *creativity, vision, idealism, imagination, compassion and determination, expanding in all directions.*

Key words:

VALUES • STRATEGY • DETAILS
ATTITUDE • ORIGINALITY

It's
all about
values

Building character is not an exact science. It is an art form. Character is built on values and emotions which are fluid, dynamic and require constant, ever-changing input in order to be maintained.

Building character requires a great deal of introspection to define our values. We will need to be very clear on what we want our public to know about us. We must let them know who we are, what we stand for and where we fit in.

Our values are the principles and standards of behaviour that guide us and shape the judgement of what is significantly important to us, those standards and behaviours which we are emotionally invested in, the ones that we want to encourage or deter. These are the principles and standards of behaviour on which we will never compromise.

When we infuse our values, both rational *(price, aesthetics, message)* and emotional *(familiar, exclusive, trustworthy)*, into our product or service, the outcome changes. They are no longer simply a product or service; they have become a brand. Now that we have a brand, our values must drive everything: the product, service, identity, reputation, visuals, expectations, the people and the actions. The challenge lies in maintaining and renewing these values over time.

Branding is the systematic approach of finding the perfect balance between rational and emotional values.

These are the values a company or organisation shares with its public: Sustainably Growing Culturally, Socially, and Financially.

DIFFERENT BY NATURE

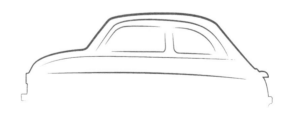

Today's world is all about accessibility. The Internet provides us with limitless information and connections, but this doesn't give us permission to be simplistic and incremental in our actions. In fact, this extreme accessibility has made the process of being original and distinctive much harder. Don't get me wrong, I'm not vilifying inspiration; quite the opposite. As creatives, we should constantly be on the lookout for endless sources of inspiration, steal as much as possible *(without plagiarizing)* and avoiding being driven by greed or laziness.

Instead, when we are looking for inspiration, let us be driven by curiosity. Ask yourself: *How could I make this better? How can I put my own twist on it? How can I develop this idea further?* The single most detrimental factor in building character is laziness.

The automotive industry is a wonderful example of how some brands mastered the ability of infusing values into a product, and others abstained from it. Simply looking at the silhouettes of different cars will immediately give us a feeling of what they stand for.

From the iconic Fiat 500 as the popular car, the indestructible VW Beetle and the rally underdog Mini Cooper, all the way to the Ferrari and its heritage in racing. Most of us inherently recognise and acknowledge the connotations of these cars in common culture; from the Lamborghini being originally designed to be the "anti-Ferrari," and the Rolls Royce, appointed as the "royal ride".

All these brands have a distinctive character, not only thanks to their outstanding products, but also to their **mastery of infusing meaning and values into their design.** Furthermore, they intentionally diverge from the masses, making them different in every feature. On the other hand, think of all those popular anonymous sedans: do they have a particular character?

a spare set of balls

of balls

保定健身球

The prospect of building a unique character can be terrifying, and building a meaningful and long lasting one even more so. If we want to create meaningful and outstanding designs and businesses, we need to push beyond our comfort zone and try something new.

As creatives, most of the time we receive phantasmagoric design briefs from our clients filled with mystical words like: "innovative," "unseen" and "creative". Then when it comes to execution, everything falls back into the safe zone, with phrases like "you know we need to keep our jobs" used to justify decisions, resulting in designers delivering the same old tired tropes again and again.

Having character requires guts, but in moderation: just enough guts to start. There is an interesting product in Chinese tradition used to improve manual dexterity and strength called the Baoding balls (保定健身球). Users start practicing with small balls by making them rotate in their palm, gradually increasing the size of the balls and speed of the rotation until the exercise is mastered.

Just like the Baoding balls, we start with a few little tasks dedicated to developing a particular character trait before progressing to being unique.

This could be anything from choosing an unconventional colour combination to using a particular finishing for our business cards. Before we know it, we will have built a mindset that is comfortably unconventional, and in doing so, we will end up with a truly unique and distinctive character.

Excellence
is a
matter of details.

Details are extremely important. Both in design and particularly in building character,

"Every detail is important because the end result is the sum of all the details involved in the creative process, no matter what we are doing". — Massimo Vignelli

From the choice of fonts to the signature of our email, from colour combinations to the texture and weight of our stationery, details are what will define our tone of voice and character. These same details and their appropriate combination will make us distinctive and unique.

In this era of physical and visual clutter, **what we feel is much more relevant than what we see.** The apparently insignificant details, those that can't be seen but definitely are perceived, are in fact the most significant.

What would Tiffany & Co be without their 1845 iconic light medium robin egg blue, or Coca-Cola without its Spencerian script and "Dynamic Ribbon Device"? Would Facebook be what it is today without its controversial "Like" button?

Now, more than ever, designs need to be sustained holistically, because regardless of style or form, **without care for details there can be no excellence.**

The ART of Strategy

Building character and crafting original designs and businesses comes neither by chance nor from a single, bright idea. It requires discipline and dedication, both supported by a well-defined strategy. Only when we have the following can we state that we are crafting a successful strategy:

   I. A clearly defined goal;
   II. A profound understanding of the overall competitive environment;
   III. A clear and objective appraisal of the available resources;
   IV. An efficient plan of action;
   V. And a unique creative vision.

Like in a sophisticated game of chess, the strategy is the way and number of moves in which we will checkmate our opponent.

We should never forget that strategy is an art! It's an expertise that is acquired through study, experience and practice. We must approach strategy with a flexible mindset and be ready to react to external conditions.

An effective strategy is about being different, which means deliberately choosing a set of activities tailored to driving us to a distinctive position. It is important to remember that the steps themselves are not the strategy. Strategy is why we do what we do, and for how long. We only have a strategy if we can maintain that distinctive position over time.

We can only implement one strategy at a time. So, we must make it the one that maximises the use of available or attainable resources without losing focus of our distinctive position.

The best strategy of all is one that changes the game, not one that tries to bend the rules in our favour. Being the best is not the point. Advancing ourselves, being better than our former self, and being unique is!

THE ESSENCE OF CHARACTER

Building character is an exercise in discipline. We must strategically define and decode which elements and values shape it.

This process requires courage and determination.

Patiently and constantly caring about the smallest details is crucial, as the end result will be the sum of them all.

MY NOTES ON CHARACTER:

DESIRE

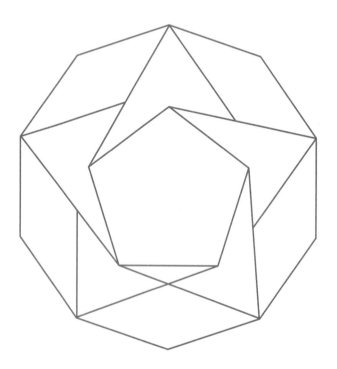

Being desirable means much more than simply being aesthetically pleasing. We must also ask ourselves: Does our design identify and solve a particular problem? How useful, usable, and accessible is the product or service we are presenting? There are two main variables that must be taken into consideration to make a product or service desirable.

First we must clearly identify what needs we are trying to satisfy and how we are enabling the public to achieve something. Second is the urge to feel. Desire is intrinsically linked to the *emotional* and *physical* bonding to the results.

In short, it is the results we crave, rather than the object per se. It is the experience of how some things will make us feel or look, and what they will enable us to achieve. It is the end result we crave, not the object.

The psychology of desire is very complex, and can range from being part of an elite to achieving social proof. The real reasons why we purchase something are more complex than simply likeability. As designers/entrepreneurs, we must distill not only the physical qualities of a product/service but also the ultimate purpose of it. I would argue that most visual and physical clutter surrounding us is the result of undefined and arbitrary design directions.

Inspiration:

I associate desire with fire 火. Our role as creatives is to develop a burning need for our product and then maintain it by constantly feeding it with creativity, just like feeding a majestic bonfire. Fire represents: *inspiration, passion, radiance, assertiveness, awareness.*

Key Words:

BEHAVIOUR • AESTHETICS • PURPOSE

CRAFTSMANSHIP • IMPACT

GOOD DESIGN CHANGES BEHAVIOUR.

Desirability is an interesting and complex topic. When we approach a new design project in the studio, we always focus on a single factor: **changing the behaviour of those who interact with our designs.**

I strongly believe that good design changes behaviour, and that, as creatives, our focus should be on understanding how the user acts now and what behaviours we want to change, enhance, discourage or disrupt.

I was in a client lobby waiting for a meeting. On the coffee table in front of me were some nicely laid out brochures and magazines. One of them was a new company profile we had just delivered to the client. I watched as another guest flicked through several brochures with one hand, not really paying attention. His flicking of the pages was automatic, subconscious even. Finally, he picked up our profile. I was eager to see his reaction.

The rigidity of the cover and choice of thicker paper forced him to use two hands, which slowed down his pace, allowing him to take in more information and really pay attention to the content of the publication.

In that moment I realised our design had changed his behaviour, and I knew we had done a good job with that product.

Whether we are working on products, brands, graphics or digital, the moral of the story is:

Approach design from a conceptual perspective rather than from a solely aesthetic one.

The dark side of design is what I call arbitrary design. Nowadays, arbitrary design takes on many forms, ranging from the misuse of 15 different fonts per page to horrific collages of cheap stock photos, to impersonal, wannabe products with ridiculously short life cycles.

More often than not, this clumsiness is a consequence of the relentless commoditisation of design. Design, rather than being a craft, has become a consumable service.

This trend is spreading so fast and through so many creative industries that I'm afraid the outstanding work of the few will be suppressed by the dark side of the many.

Design involves **gaining a deep understanding of who we are before** and who we will be **after** applying a design solution. Only then will we be able to craft the outer expression of the character that will infuse our design, ultimately making it desirable to the greater public.

Everyone wants to be Nike, Apple, Gucci, but how many are willing to operate at the same standard as these companies do? Are they willing to dedicate the same resources? Are they willing to take the same risks?

No design process should be commoditised or made arbitrary. When we do so, we are left with mere caricatures of who we really are. I understand that being a compromised version of someone else is attractive and can even be charming. That's the draw of the dark side. **We should always strive to be the best version of ourselves.** Great design is never arbitrary! As designers, we must consciously and discernibly present solutions in the simplest, most understandable and aesthetically pleasing way possible.

An old engineer once taught me that: "*There are only two kinds of design: design that works and design that doesn't work*".

CARE

CREATE AESTHETICALLY REWARDING EXPERIENCES

In classical philosophy, Plato argued that beautiful objects carefully incorporate **proportion, harmony,** and **unity.** Similarly, Aristotle found that the universal elements of beauty were **order, symmetry,** and **definiteness (clarity).**

All these elements are extremely important and represent the foundation of good design. So make this your best practice: Look at your design project and, ask yourself if the design is **harmonious, ordered** and **defined.** If the answer is no, I strongly recommend you go back to the drawing board.

If the answer is yes, don't kick back and relax just yet there are still a few more things to think about. As we develop a new design concept, we must **transcend** the purely **functional** and **aesthetic** value of design, focusing on **crafting the overall experience** around a product or service. We must meticulously analyse every point of interaction between our design and the user. These touchpoints are an opportunity to imprint our core values, status, beliefs and meaning.

If we pay for an expensive dinner, we don't just expect food of outstanding quality, but also presentation, service, and environment.

Similarly, we should not approach design as a static discipline. The interaction between a product and a user is a dynamic, complex process. Aesthetics are only one of the components of the experience, albeit an important one, and one that certainly plays a fundamental role in the early stages of interaction. Despite aesthetics' significance, we must also be aware of all the other elements that come into play in the interaction, such as **message, environment, service and status.**

Nowadays, it is not good enough to merely present a pleasant product or service. We must fanatically C.A.R.E. *(Create Aesthetically Rewarding Experiences)* for the overall experience that surrounds our design, because if we as creators don't, then why should anyone else?

GOOD ENOUGH IS NOT ENOUGH

There is a specific expression in Mandarin that intrigues me: Chà Bu Duō (差不多).

Depending on its context, "Chà Bu Duō" can be translated as close enough, almost, just about, or approximately. Translated literally, it means: *Difference not much*. Particularly in creative fields, this expression can act as the portrayal of a disastrous attitude, leading to the creation of a final product or service that is only "Chà Bu Duō - Good Enough!"

At this point you may be questioning the focus on "bad" design habits. It comes down to one thing: subjectivity.

It is very difficult to express an objective point of view when talking about desirability, but what we can successfully do is analyse bad habits or inappropriate behaviours and try to avoid them. This is how we eventually become more sophisticated designers.

So what are the causes of bad design? After investing a considerable amount of time into analysing my own design projects that fell short and asking a few respected designers and creatives that same simple question, three common factors emerged:

I. PURPOSE — LACK OF VISION

We often forget that the greatest creations served a higher purpose: The colosseum (Amphitheatrum Flavium) was not only a stadium, it was a physical representation of the Roman Empire's greatness.

II. CRAFTSMANSHIP — LACK OF MEANINGFUL DETAILS

When we are pressured by a tight deadline, we compromise both craft and principles, losing sight of the meaningful details.

III. IGNORANCE — LACK OF COMPREHENSIVE KNOWLEDGE

*When we don't have enough knowledge on the subject matter and heedlessly throw things together, we forget our duty to create something of **irreducible complexity**.*

These are the attributes that lead us into the "Chà Bu Duō" trap. This is when we set the stage for what will almost certainly be a colossal fiasco. Believe me, I've done it many times.

So before developing our design solution, let's take a moment to ask ourselves the following:

I. Are we designing for the right reasons? Is our design serving a **deeper purpose** with a **meaningful** and **forward-looking vision**?

II. Are we ready to passionately pay attention and dedicate ourselves to the project? Are we going to care about even minor details?

III. Do we have all the necessary knowledge and resources to create a project that is remarkable and unique?

This simple, humbling act of questioning ourselves is already setting us up for success.

Don't forget: **good enough is no longer enough**.

Make it **20%**
BETTER

The title statement might sound contradicting and puzzling, and it should. Aren't we as designers, innovators, entrepreneurs supposed to think big and change the world? Yes! 20% at a time.

For most of my career, this has been, and still is, one of my guiding principles. I look at something *(especially so if it is a design or product I truly admire or despise)* and ask myself: **How would I make this better?** In the spirit of fighting arbitrariness, I began asking myself what **"better"** truly means to me. So I start analysing the product or design a bit deeper. To truly understand what will make it **better.** There is a fascinating principle that might help us solve the riddle.

The Pareto principle, also known as the 80–20 rule, the law of the vital few, and the principle of factor sparsity. It states that: **For many events, roughly 80% of the effects come from 20% of the causes.** In design, we can translate this to mean that 20% of the traits of the analysed design will be responsible for 80% of the impact of the design's overall success. Life isn't fair and this principle reinforces the fact that most things in life *(effort, reward, output)* are not distributed evenly. Some contribute more than others.

So if we can identify the 20% of the traits that generate the **greater impact**, N.B. greater impact not total impact the number could be 80/20, 90/10, or 90/20 the core is to identify what **causes** generate **most of** the **effects** on the desirability of our design, we should be able to understand what actions might be taken to make it better.

For example, if we are about to redesign a marmalade jar, we should start by identifying the top ten traits that make our jar iconic. These could be [1] *form*, [2] *label*, [3] *typography*, [4] *image*, [5] *message*, [6] *lid*, [7] *product reveal*, [8] *colour*, [9] *texture*, and [10] *materiality*. Now that we have analysed all the key traits, can we identify the two that **need the most improvement or radical change?** If we correctly address these two main issues, there is a good chance the overall design will be **"better"**.

I know this example might seem a bit simplistic, but believe me, it's a very practical exercise and has served me well so far. The process of constraining myself to identify the two or the few most significant traits of a product or design is the method that truly pushes me to find a creative solution.

I believe that
true creativity comes from constraints.

Freedom and creativity are two very different things. **Boundaries, limits and constraints are the true driving force behind creativity and innovation.** Pushing ourselves to bend or overcome those constraints creates the foundation for true creative and innovative thinking. This is where needs and desire successfully unite.

THE ESSENCE OF DESIRE

Being desirable is much more than being solely aesthetically pleasing.

We must Create Aesthetically Rewarding Experiences (C.A.R.E.) that change the behaviour of our target.

We shall design with purpose, care for meaningful details and have comprehensive knowledge of the subject matter.

We must always fight arbitrariness, while developing

the outer expression of our distinctive character.

NEVER fall into the trap of being superficial. Exceed expectations. Strive to fulfill a real need.

Know that some factors contribute more than others to the desirability of a product or service.

Finally, always design to trigger basic human emotions.

MY NOTES ON DESIRE:

EMPATHY

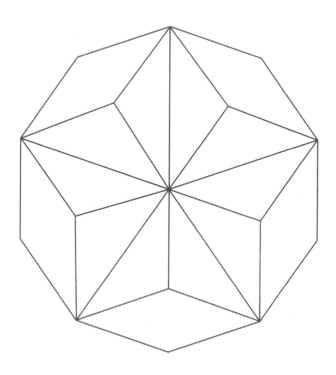

To infuse meaning into our designs, we must share and communicate values and distinctive points to the public. It is essential that we take a new approach in the way we communicate with the public.

These days, it is not enough to limit communication to describing a product or service. It has become vital to engage the public on a **deeper level** with the hopes of creating a strong sense of empathy.

Consumers no longer want to simply buy a product or service. They want to feel part of a special community. They want to be involved on ground level with the "inner crowd" while the product acts as a badge or icon that grants them access to that special community.

From customers to employees, it is essential to engage everyone in the design process, making them feel part of something greater than just a commercial transaction. Never forget that **companies are social institutions just as much as financial ones.**

Inspiration:

I associate empathy with earth ⊥. It is our duty to create an environment (soil) in which our communication can be deeply rooted. A rich and solid foundation provides a platform for our design to grow taller and stronger.

Earth represents: *generosity, thoughtfulness, transformation, practicality and stability.*

Key words:

TARGET • NEEDS • STORIES

COMMUNITY • RECOGNITION

2

10

28

60

78

82

The Supreme Quest of Alchemy

Before chemistry was a science, there was alchemy. One of the supreme quests of alchemy was to transmute lead into gold. Lead *(atomic number 82)* and gold *(atomic number 79)* are defined as elements by the number of protons they possess.

Therefore, changing an element requires changing its atomic number *(+/- protons)*. The number of protons cannot be altered by chemical means. However, physics may be used to add or remove protons, and thereby change one element *(lead)* into another *(gold)*. Being a very stable element, forcing lead to release three protons (82-79 = 3) requires a vast amount of energy, so much so that the cost of transmuting it greatly surpasses the value of the resulting gold.

So what can we learn from this alchemic quest?

I. Yes, almost everything is possible. *But is it worth it?*

II. Working with something already valuable is easier than trying to modify something that isn't.

III. So, you want to sell lead for gold. *Are you willing to pay the absurdly high price that comes with it?*

Whether we are looking at the intrinsic value of a product or how valuable our consumers are, **we should accept reality as it is, not as we want it to be.** Gold is gold, lead is lead, just like a good product is good and a poor one is poor.

There is a very low probability that our design will appeal to everyone. Trying to sell something of little value (or trying to sell something to someone who does not perceive its value) is almost impossible. However, if our heart is set on that goal, we should be prepared to pay the price. **Pleasing everyone will result in pleasing no one,** and eventually, only create mundane solutions. In other words, 1. Don't sell crap, and 2. Don't try to sell to those who don't care.

DON'T
SELL

INSPIRE

If we want our target to care about our design, we have to care about them first. Caring means constantly understanding and sharing the feelings of our target audience; inspiring them and being inspired by them.

The word *"inspire"* is derived from the Latin *"inspirare"*, which means to "breathe or blow into". We must whisper the secrets of our design to consumers, and how our product can **make them more productive, have better style, be healthier,** or whatever our product or service ultimately **promises to do for them.**

Great brands don't focus on the technical strength, durability, or price of their product, but instead inspire us with astonishing images of travel, empowerment, adventure and love for craftsmanship.

They inspire us to **become someone else:** a traveler, an athlete, a rock-star, and eventually, **a better version of ourselves.**

In turn, we must be inspired by our target, watching as they react to our design. Great brands seldom concentrate their communications solely on the technical features of a product or service, but mostly on how the consumers use and embrace their products.

One of the most devastating behaviours for a company is to **lose connection with its core target** by trying to chase a mainstream market. The mainstream market is hard to inspire considering its diversity and size. It's relatively easy to communicate to them, but increasingly difficult to inspire them.

This analysis does not apply solely to high-end products or brands. It can be applied to every single product or service, even the most mundane. Inspiration doesn't have to mean glittering fancy words. It can also be an honest, straightforward tap on the shoulder.

FOLLOW TO LEAD

LEAD TO FOLLOW

We all know that creating a strong community of true believers isn't easy. Can you recall the last time you tried to organise a dinner for 10? Was it challenging? What about raising money for a good cause? How hard is it to inspire and connect with more than a handful of friends?

Establishing a significant movement is feasible and extremely gratifying. The initial step is to change our mindset and understand the real dynamics behind how a community is created. First things first: as leaders we must be **fearless** and **accept criticism.** If we are not polarising people, we aren't worthy of their attention and they will understandably forget us.

Once we have found our true believers *(ourselves, our employees, our friends and family)*, we have to **show them how to follow us,** while still embracing them as equals.

Being complacent about or underestimating our first followers, or early adopters, is a sign of bad leadership and poor vision. Look closely at situations where a community is to be established and you will find that new **followers often emulate other followers rather than the leader.**

Once this happens, it is no longer about **us** or **our product.** It is **about the community** and how members connect with each other. A strong community is built on Andy showing Patrick how to solve his problems with the help of our product or service.

This is the core of creating empathy: **connecting** with people and **solving their problems.** Give them a **reason to gather;** have the courage to **follow** and **show others how to follow.**

Before we know, we will have a community of true believers, and our product will be the icon or badge that **grants** them **access** to this **special community.**

WE ARE ALL NATURAL BORN STORY-TELLERS

As people, we are all fundamentally different, except for when it comes to our expectations as consumers. None of us enjoy passively accepting whatever is offered to us. We demand to be **entertained, satisfied** and **surprised.** In other words, we need to be involved.

As designers and entrepreneurs, we must become expert storytellers if we want our public to be engaged and supportive of our quests. We must create a story or message that can be easily spread.

This message should be **essential, concrete,** and **credible.** It should be solid enough to withstand word-of-mouth exchanges without losing its essence, but at the same time be fluid enough to withstand personalisation as it spreads.

A well-thought-out message should stimulate the public's curiosity and exceed their expectations while also being easily understandable and motivational enough to encourage people to spread the word.

Here are the top 8 components that make a great story. They are tips I have collected from some of the world's best storytellers:

I.   Create a promise that engages the public emotionally, intellectually and aesthetically;

II. Clearly define a strong theme that runs throughout the story;

III. Present the "itch" you can't scratch, which can be something audience can relate to;

IV. Build a scene rife with anticipation, mingled with uncertainty;

V.   Infuse mystery through a well-organised absence of information and allow the audience to do the math;

VI. Invoke wonder by using an active voice;

VII. Express your core values and beliefs by focusing on the essentials;

VIII. Find a physical trigger that will work with your story.

Building a compelling story is not an easy task, but it is definitely one of the most important. Whether we are preparing for a pitch, a manifesto to publish on our website, or simply drafting our elevator speech, the core message and story that we share with our public is among the first points of contact.

A simpler structure we can start practising with is a 3-step pitch or story:

I.   Start with a clear, declarative sentence about your company, service or product and what it stands for;

II. Support the declarative sentence with 3 key facts or benefits about your company, service or product;

III. Reinforce the 3 benefits with stories, statistics, and examples.

Finally, I would like to share the same advice an old friend gave me while starting my academic career:

If you want people to truly learn a subject you must: Tell them, Show them, and Let them practice.

PRACTISE YOUR STORYTELLING

CORE STATEMENT:

_____

_____

_____

THREE BENEFITS:

1. _____

2. _____

3. _____

BENEFIT 1 – SUPPORT STORY:

_____

_____

_____

BENEFIT 2 – SUPPORT STORY:

_____

_____

_____

BENEFIT 3 – SUPPORT STORY:

_____

_____

_____

PUT EVERYTHING TOGETHER IN 50-60 WORDS:

_____

_____

_____

_____

_____

A
SYMB☮L
A
MANTRA

MAKE LOVE NOT WAR

A

rejects the mores of established society
and advocates a nonviolent ethic

CAUSE

The pinnacle of empathy is **the unique identity we can provide for our community.** There is nothing more powerful than the manifestation of membership, be it a common culture, jargon, theme, colour scheme or style.

It is essential that our target feels like part of an exclusive group. It must be clear when you are a part of the inner crowd and when you are not. We are all social animals; it is embedded in our DNA. Our survival instinct leads us to gather for a particular purpose or activity. This dates back to the stone age, when groups gathered for reasons like hunting mammoth.

It is not always necessary to be extreme *(such as by growing a beard or wearing an eye patch)*, but it is very important that we provide our newly established community with **a symbol of belonging.** Think of significant movements and trends like the Hippies, Punks, Yuppies and Hipsters, and see if this applies.

We begin with **a cause.** This is where we have to get our community to believe what we believe.

We reinforce with **a mantra.** This is where we provide our following with a mission to accomplish. A mantra is not a tagline. A mantra is what we stand for — "why" we exist *(i.e. a mantra for Nike would be: empowering athletes. Its tagline is: Just Do It)*.

Finally, we provide a unique identity, **a symbol.** It could be a pin, a sticker, a way of talking. This is the trademark of belonging to that inner crowd, and being a part of the inner crowd, any inner-crowd at all, is cool.

THE ESSENCE OF EMPATHY

It is our duty as designers and entrepreneurs to care for and engage with our public on a deeper level.

First we need to find the real lovers, the true believers. It is onto this audience that we shall focus our efforts.

These are the people worthy of our attention and love. These are the people we must lead, coach and follow.

We must provide them with a cause, a reason to believe, and make them an essential part of our mission.

We must inspire them with wonder, allow them to be part of our design philosophy and let them carry our message, using it as a way to connect with others.

MY NOTES ON EMPATHY:

TRUST

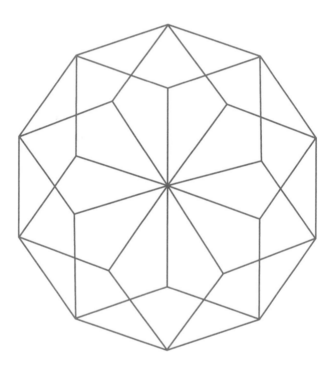

Trust is inarguably the most complex and controversial of all five principles. Harder to earn and much easier to lose, building trust requires the investment of time and effort.

The aim is always to become reliable and maintain values and promises by delivering more than expected. It is a fact that today's customers tend to be more disloyal than in the past, thanks to a profusion of choices and too little time.

Moreover, most products filling store shelves have similar qualities and features which are also often inconsistent with their function or market.

This leaves customers with "price" as their only reliable selection criteria.

On the other hand, a choice based on trust has entirely different dynamics: our beloved brand must be familiar without being dull, innovative without being risky, and authentic without being inaccessible.

Inspiration:

I associate trust with metal *(gold)* 金. In the same way that a smith handles real metal, we must forge a brand, product or business that never compromises on core values, that remains as untarnishable as pure gold and as strong as steel.

Metal represents: *discipline, solidity, and steadfastness.*

Key Words:

COMPETENT • HONEST • RELIABLE
AUTHENTIC • FAMILIAR

THE TRUST SPIRAL

Building trust is not a single act. It is an enduring process that must be repeated over and over just like a never-ending cycle. Here is one way the trust cycle can be broken:

A company fails to deliver quality as it chases a greater margin; the public then reacts by choosing the cheapest player in order to reduce risk; that way, if the company doesn't deliver, at least not much has been lost.

The company then counteracts and cuts investments to increase profitability and so on and so forth, inevitably creating an endless downward spiral.

This "cheaper price" war is extremely unhealthy for both industries and consumers. To fix it, we must revert the spiral into a **virtuous, empowering trust cycle.**

The single most important question we should ask ourselves is not how to gain the public's trust, but **how to become trustworthy.**

Trust is granted to us by other people. We can't force anyone to give trust, and we can't simply state that we are trustworthy. We can only provide **tangible evidence** to support this declaration.

A brand, company or product fails to deliver when it doesn't genuinely intend to express **its true qualities** and **values** by demonstrating how the design or product can **positively impact the customer's life** and what it **enables them to achieve.** This can include being the most affordable product on the market; think Best Buy, Walmart or IKEA. Being affordable is part of their DNA.

That simple change of mindset, going from gaining trust to **becoming trustworthy,** is the first turning point of the trust spiral.

TIME
IS
MONEY,
BUT
MONEY
IS **NOT**
TIME

People will believe we are trustworthy if we can demonstrate three key qualities:

I. **Competence:** Having the necessary ability, knowledge, or skill to do something successfully;

II. **Honesty:** Acting truthfully, with sincerity and keeping our word;

III. **Reliability:** Consistently delivering both quality and performance.

To further explain these qualities, I often use a controversial example. To me, McDonald's is trustworthy, at least in all the ways that matter for their market.

I don't trust that McDonald's will serve me nouvelle cuisine, but I do trust that it will deliver almost the same taste, all over the world, at an affordable price.

By doing so, their core promises remain clear: Standard Quality, Prime Locations, Affordable Price.

They also leverage another important attribute of trust, which is familiarity, by dedicating an incredible amount of time and resources towards becoming **familiar** and **accessible**.

It's true that you can buy familiarity by pushing your image out there. But cold cash alone won't do the trick.

The time a company or brand **invests in the relationship with their clients** in order to reinforce its values is **priceless**, and this process can seldom be purchased.

The Power of PLAY

In the field of creativity and innovation, playing is a serious matter. Over the past few years my mission has been to form creative minds and help companies, organisations and entrepreneurs transform ideas into realities.

Unfortunately, most of the time this process is so mechanized and stiff that we lose the poetry and beauty that comes with the creation of a new product, service or venture. There is a wonderful quote that truly inspires me:

> *"The master in the art of living makes little distinction between his work and his play, his labor and his leisure, his mind and his body, his information and his recreation, his love and his religion.*
> *He hardly knows which is which.*
> *He simply pursues his vision of excellence at whatever he does, leaving others to decide whether he is working or playing. To him, he's always doing both."*
>
> L.P. Jacks

We tend to forget that at the end of the day, what really matters is not always the winning or losing. In design it's all about playing the game, and staying in the game for as long as possible.

Playing the game means **constantly advancing ourselves, pursuing our vision of excellence** in whatever we do. Our personal advancement will ultimately translate into **creating value for our stakeholders.**

Playing doesn't mean not taking something seriously. In fact, it can mean pretty much the opposite. Even when kids are playing, maybe building a construction, they can take this task very seriously because **they want to succeed,** not win. They want to **advance and learn something new.**

The huge difference between an operational mindset and a playful mindset is **the approach to failure.** With an operational mindset, failure is shameful, while a playful one gives us the freedom to fail and retry. It gives us permission *(confidence and trust)* to start over and seek different results.

Having a playful mindset enables us to improve our skills and performances. Continuous learning is the secret to excelling in something, as well as reducing the probability of error. When we embrace a playful mindset, we consider the error an essential part of learning, not a demonstration of incompetence.

We will learn in the following chapters that failure is something we must embrace and capitalize upon. This can only be achieved if we understand the power of a playful mindset.

There are a few simple steps we can take to start changing our mindset from operational to playful.

I. Understand which game we are playing.

As brilliantly explained by Simon Sinek in one of his talks, the first step is to understand which game we are playing. In game theory, there are two types of games: finite games and infinite games. A finite game is defined as having known players, fixed rules and an agreed-upon objective.

Soccer is a good example of a finite game. The players know each other, the rules, and have agreed that whichever team has the most goals after ninety minutes plus extra time wins the game.

Alternatively an infinite game is characterised by having both known and unknown players, changeable rules and the objective is to **perpetuate the game for as long as possible.** In an infinite game there is no winner or loser; players only drop out when they lose the will or resources to continue. In other words, finite players are playing to win and infinite players are playing to stay in the game.

If we are playing a finite game, first of all we must make sure it truly is finite. We must be absolutely certain we master all the rules, know who the players and leaders are, and the ultimate goal of the game.

If we are playing an infinite game (such as business, or even more so business design), the goal is to stay in the game for as long as possible. We must be mindful of the necessary resources needed to stay in the game and constantly advance, becoming a better version ourself and focusing every day on excelling in our craft.

II. Run reality checks often.
A playful mindset embraces reality as is and also understands the need for continuous new input. There will always be something new we need to know about a topic or subject. A good and thorough reality check will help us identify the obstacles we need to overcome and, even more importantly, identify the people or groups we need to work with to achieve our goal.

III. Change the direction, not the goal.
To cite Confucius: *"When it is obvious that the goals cannot be reached, don't adjust the goals, adjust the action steps."*

This leads back to our original topic of failure. It doesn't matter how challenging our goal is, there will always be a way to achieve it. It may be that the very first approach we take will not be the correct one, but here is where our playful mindset kicks in. We must change our vocabulary to achieve that; problems become challenges, failures become tests, improvements become next steps and perfection becomes excellence.

These three simple steps are the very foundation of changing our habits and shifting to a playful mindset.

How do we become trustworthy?
The obvious answer is:

We should try to get as much exposure as possible, because the more people know us, the more products we can sell.

Being solely visible was a tactic that worked 50 years ago, and it's no longer sufficient. If we truly want people to trust us, we must give them adequate, useful, and **tangible evidence** that we are trustworthy.

We must also be contextually relevant, which means **being aware of the underlying culture that surrounds us.** We must connect and communicate what is of interest to our target.

We must **understand how and where our message will be consumed,** and most importantly, **when our audience will be ready to listen.**

There is a host of ways to demostrate that we are trustworthy, yet so far the most effective one I've found is to be **open, connected,** and **vulnerable.** Being ready for the possibility of being attacked, criticised or harmed, either physically or emotionally, is a good sign of trustworthiness and confidence.

This may sound insanely risky, but it's not. The more **relevantly connected** we are, the more people will trust us. If we are afraid of connecting or being criticised, it is because we either have something to hide or we don't believe in what we do. If this is the case, it is time to reconsider our core values.

WHAT ABOUT WHAT WE ARE LOSING

When it comes to trust, what we don't do has just as much impact as what we do. Many companies I have worked with did everything just right. They crafted a good product and image, had a fair presence both on- and offline, yet they still struggled to develop a strong relationship with their customers. Putting all these experiences together, I noticed one common mistake: a narrow focus on only certain activities which can be measured in terms of retention or ROI.

Some examples include: *"If we send this email, how many new subscribers can we get...?"* or *"If we do this event, how many customers can we engage?"* and so on.

If we give in to this mindset, we will develop a sort of tunnel vision which will limit our ability to discover and evaluate other new and exciting possibilities. So, instead of focusing on how much we can gain, I suggest thinking **about the costs of a missed opportunity.**

For example: *"If we fail to serve one customer, how many potential customers will this affect?"* or *"If we don't have a good functional website, how many netizens are we losing?"*

This approach will drastically change our attitude to how we might develop and market a new brand or design. As we start to look for more viable and valuable solutions, we open our mind to a broader vision.

This is also great practice to keep our design fresh, while others might struggle to keep up with the increasing pace of the competition.

THE ESSENCE OF TRUST

Trust is much more about us than it is about them.

It's about giving rather than taking. We don't take trust from others, we develop and demonstrate that we are trustworthy.

To do so we must give tangible evidence of trustworthiness.

We must become familiar and reliable while being clear about what we stand for and never lose a chance to demonstrate that.

We must keep a playful mindset, focusing on being open, connected and relevant.

MY NOTES ON TRUST:

CONSISTENCY

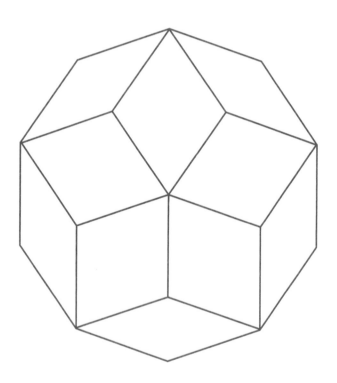

L ast but not least, consistency is the place where everything begins and ends. We live in a hectic world, and a single, brilliant idea may not be enough to ensure sustainable, long-lasting growth.

Rather than rely on a stroke of genius, we must consistently distinguish ourselves from the crowd. To be desirable on different levels, we need to engage the public with a compelling story, make them feel like they are part of the journey, and seek to renew trust by providing evidence of our competence and reliability.

Consistency means having the ability to be **essential**, **concrete** and **credible** over time, **never compromising** on our **core values** and yet always renewing ourselves.

We must also be able to distinguish between image and identity. The secret to achieving this is to keep all elements aligned and monitored.

Inspiration:

Design and business are organic processes, not static ones. They are as fluid as water 水 Water represents: *willpower, magnetism, sensitivity, wisdom and persuasiveness.*

Key Words:

IMAGE & IDENTITY • HUMAN CENTRED • COLLABORATIVE • EXPERIMENTAL • STATUS

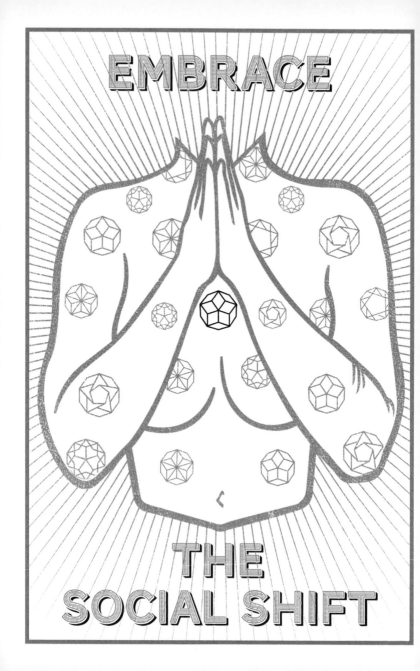

There is a reason why design and branding are such important topics and arguably two of the most significant strategical assets in a company today.

In the past few years, a social shift has occurred: from an industrial society, where the general public acknowledged the functional value of a product, to a postmodern society, where the general public acknowledges the symbolic value of a product.

As argued by Alain de Botton in his book *Status Anxiety*, "Much of the reason we go shopping is unconnected to any urgent material need. [...] We often shop for emotional, rather than practical reasons. A lot of consumption is about acquiring status symbols [...] and material objects whose primary use is psychological rather than functional".

They are objects that signal to the world we are worthy of dignity and respect. We must embrace and understand this shift, because solely producing products or services is no longer enough!

We have to start creating status symbols. This means crafting not just the product or service, but the overall culture that surrounds it.

I believe we *(entrepreneurs, design professionals, creative minds)* should strive to infuse deep cultural and social value into our work. When crafting something, we must inspire people who interact with our work to know and feel that they are not just buying another piece of merchandise. Instead, they should perceive the acquisition of new knowledge, a fragment of culture.

THE

HOW

IS AS IMPORTANT AS

THE

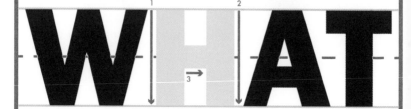

WHAT

Far too many times I have been asked to give the secret recipe for creating luxury brands or award-winning products, when there is none! Most of the time I instead find myself reminding people that how we achieve something is just as important as the outcome.

There are serious implications that stem from the methods we use to achieve something. Timeless design and brands usually have a specific journey that is as attractive as the actual product or service they present.

Sometimes it's their heritage or a particular production process; other times it's the journey of the founder. Either way, it always comes down to how the customer feels and how they share those feelings with others.

As we embrace this philosophy, we start to see that **the development process is just as valuable as the outcome** itself. Big or small, every step changes how we arrive at our destination, and we can learn more from the process than from the outcome.

Remember, if the process doesn't add value to what we are doing, then inevitably the outcome will lose value we never even knew it had.

To me, **design is** far more **experimental** than it is predefined. I try as much as I can never to fall in love with the very first ideas, as that wouldn't allow **the design process to guide** me to the end solution.

The final outcome might vary or be unsatisfactory due to many variables, and that's why **we must fall in love with the process, not the outcome.**

THE BEAUTY
OF
SUSTAINABLE
FAILURE

What is the key to consistent improvement? What are the obstacles we have to overcome to be original and unique? While strolling at the mall or casually surfing the web, I often get frustrated and think, *"How is it possible that so many brands produce items with little to no difference between them?"* My conclusion is fear. These brands fear failure so much they clone one another, naively thinking this is the safer choice.

We shouldn't be afraid of failure. We should accept and embrace failure as an essential part of the learning process.

Sustainable failure always identifies the next step. If we haven't learned anything from our failure *(and therefore can't identify what our next step is)*, then we are just being incremental, or hoping for a cheap win from a mundane solution. To embrace failure with confidence, we must first identify in which areas we can afford errors, and in which ones we absolutely cannot afford to fail. In Japanese culture there is a fascinating philosophy called ***Kintsugi*** *(golden joinery)*. The antique Japanese art of restoring broken or damaged pottery with lacquer dusted or mixed with powdered gold, silver, or platinum. This philosophy treats breakage and repair as part of the history of an object, rather than something to disguise, a perfect example of embracing the beauty of failure.

A sports analogy we can all understand is tennis: *In the first serve, players give all they have, trying to score an ace. If that fails, the second serve becomes much more strategical. Players read the opponent, evaluate weak spots and use a more sophisticated but safer technique to score.* They embrace the beauty of sustainable failure.

Let's say we are launching a new product. *We know we can't fail in core functionality or target, but we might try a daring colour combination which we suspect might not appeal to the greater masses*. At least we will then stand out from the crowd and know what our next step will be. Try it!

We will soon discover that the knowledge we gain from failure is actually greater than any of the initial frustration.

One of the most common misconceptions with regards to consistency is the all-paralysing fear of change, as many companies tend to confuse consistency with lethargy.

The consequence of this attitude is inevitably becoming obsolete and commonplace as they can't seem to distinguish between image and identity.

I once asked a top manager at Hermès how they maintain such consistency across all their communications without ever being boring or dull. This was his response:

"As we develop products and images, the essence must be there with or without our logo; we are always unmistakably Hermès in every detail. From our choice of colours to the quality of paper we use in our bags and boxes, to the embroidered ribbons that are regularly redesigned to reflect different themes.

Put simply, we always express art, craftsmanship and elegance. These are our core values and we never compromise on them. The rest is just make-up".

The essential duality in every brand, business or design exists between its IMAGE, a representation of its external form, and its IDENTITY, the sum of characteristics determining who or what that brand or design is.

In other words:
Image is how we look.
Identity is what we stand for.

DESIGN THINKING
×
DESIGNERS

IMPLEMENTATION

INSPIRATION

EXPERIMENTAL

HUMAN CENTRED

COLLABORATIVE

IDEATION

One of the most fascinating aspects of design is the ever-changing nature of this profession. 50 years ago, design was very different from what it is today, and I'm excited to think of what it will become in the next 50 years.

That said, the past can be just as fascinating, and it's astonishing how little we ponder on it. Maybe that is the reason I titled this book *Timeless*. It's impossible to accurately predict what design will be in 50 or 100 years, but one thing remains certain: what was valuable 500 years ago is still relevant today, more than ever. To quote the greatest design thinker of all time:

> *" Nature must be your guide ... Nature begins with a cause and ends with an experience. So begin with the experience and then investigate the cause. "*

— *Leonardo da Vinci, Manuscript E, folio 55r, circa 1513–1514*

I have attended several workshops where "Design Thinking" is reduced to a gimmicky step-by-step linear process that promises to boost creativity rather than understand the very foundations of design itself.

When the foundations and underlying principles of design thinking are not clearly understood and embraced, the process becomes tedious and, quite frankly, a little frustrating. So let's begin by understanding the three main pillars of design thinking:

I. **Human centered:** Design must address basic human needs, taking into consideration the different contexts of where and how a design solution is applied, and culminating in a practical, tangible solution.

II. **Experimental:** The process is not a predetermined sequence of events, but rather an organic conversation. We sketch what we know and quickly respond to those marks, constructing something which hopefully we've never seen before. To validate those ideas, we create prototypes, often exploring and deconstructing problems to generate new solutions previously unknown to us. We embrace failure as an indication of the next step, not as a demonstration of incompetence.

III. **Collaborative:** In design we embrace subjectivity, and understand that many new ideas are simply variations or combinations of existing ones. This helps avoid idea fixation. Design is truly multidisciplinary. We recognize the power of a holistic solution that unfolds itself in every part of the process.

Nowadays, design has more in common with the direction of a piece of musical work than a simple trade/production of goods: multiple players with very specific scores need to perfectly execute their part so that the ultimate result is a harmonious and precise performance. Design is a common language between all parties, from production to distribution to sales.

The underlying power of good design is the ability to offer a means of increasing understanding and building consensus in a complex world. It is a way to **accelerate the adoption of an idea.** Design's ultimate goal is to **create a cohesive culture** that grants meaning, not only to our words and drawings, but also to people's emotional and rational intellect.

Good design has the ability to involve each party in its creation, ideally in equally relevant ways. The common impression should be that the design has become a work of art in which all parties have played a role.

The ideal state is a harmonious performance of many parts, just like an orchestra that plays well together. Our role as designers, entrepreneurs and creatives is to meticulously compose the symphony before distributing a **clear, simple,** and **agreed-upon** score.

When this happens, a design, business or brand is not only **prosperous,** but also **beautiful.**

As I mentioned at the beginning of this book, the lines between product design, graphic design, branding, marketing, advertising and business in general are blurring.

Therefore, we have to approach **business design as a holistic practice** in which the whole is different from the sum of its parts. We must regard it as a complex system in which relationships are key. It is the connections and relationships between all these parts that define why and how a complex system such as business design works.

THE ESSENCE OF CONSISTENCY

Being consistent doesn't mean being static; quite the opposite.

When our core values are solid, we can be formless and shapeless, adapting to different conditions without ever losing our essence.

Our solutions must be human centred, experimental and collaborative.

Consistency allows us to deal with variability and choice.

Avoid subjectivity in design choices but embrace it in regards to our target.

The complexity of design reveals itself as we create a variety of different solutions for a variety of different targets.

Therefore, appropriateness and discipline are extremely important, but so is ambiguity.

MY NOTES ON CONSISTENCY:

FINAL
THOUGHTS

THE BEAUTY OF COMPLEXITY

I find it puzzling that the more complex and competitive our world becomes, the more simplistic and mundane our solutions are.

There is an intrinsic beauty in complexity— in the process of thinking deeply about a problem and then exploring, evaluating, and testing the most appropriate solution.

There is beauty in a well-crafted thought, a deeply intense elaboration and a sophisticated line of reasoning.

There is beauty in caring for the apparently insignificant details that can't be seen but can definitely be perceived.

And there is beauty in the maniacal search for the most suited solution after a frustrating series of failures.

I must admit that I'm terrified by the inadequacy and thoughtlessness with which we approach complex problems nowadays. I always try to create work with deep social and cultural meaning, and believe this is what will set us apart from the crowd.

OBLIGATION TO SIMPLICITY

One of the most fascinating paradoxes in design and business in particular is that the more complex and profound a concept is, the simpler we must express it.

This is our duty as entrepreneurs and designers: making something remarkable accessible to many, and positively impacting their lives.

The ultimate sophistication is presenting a complex and meaningful product or service in the simplest way possible. If we fully embrace the beauty of complexity, the expression of simplicity will reveal itself almost naturally.

The little things are the ones that create a great difference— be it the three clicks of an iPod, the distinctive sound of a guitar in a group of musicians, or the use of a particular spice from a famous chef.

The small details, the simple ones, are the ones that hold great force. Obligation to simplicity is the foundation of respecting our customer base.

When our values are simple, clear and understandable, our users will embrace our design as their own and that is what really matters.

A LOOK AT THE FUTURE,
A THOUGHT TO THE PAST

Is it still possible to create truly meaningful and timeless designs even in the complex world we live in today? I believe so.

 Design is an exercise in dedication, love, care, and discipline. It is an exercise in researching the perfect synthesis between value, meaning, harmony, and proportion. I believe this to be the foundation for crafting a successful, meaningful and timeless design.

The more access to information we have and the more globally connected our world becomes, the more we tend to disregard a product's place of origin, heritage, or craftsmanship. Sad, but true. Even if we would like to capitalise on them, none of these attributes are valuable if they aren't appropriately expressed, contextualised, and even more importantly, shared with the public.

It is essential to understand that design must shape cultures rather that just generate visual or physical clutter. While there are important differences between each and every market or target, there are many philosophical concerns that transcend cultural differences, and there is much to be gained from seeing familiar problems in a new way.

As designers, we must embrace the dynamism of the world we live in. This shouldn't be an excuse to be incremental and commonplace, though even if low hanging fruits are temptingly placed at the ends of our fingertips.

We must rediscover the greatness and refined sophistication that was once a distinctive point of pride in our craft.

There is so much more to it—than creating simple merchandise or performing a task. We must realise that the most important objects and experiences surrounding us are the ones that positively impact our lives. Those are the meaningful and timeless objects and experiences truly reflecting the candid story of who we are. These are the kinds of objects and experiences we should strive to create.

As a creative professional and educator, my job is to look at things and constantly ask myself, *how can I make them better?* My real job is not to create pretty logos, fancy books or sexy packaging. It is truly to awaken possibility in other people, to honour great design and form talented designers for their future careers.

I believe that as designers, entrepreneurs and creatives, we share an enormous responsibility. We are responsible for crafting the messages and visions about what the world is now, and what it should aspire to be.

THE END

APPLYING THE MODEL

A SIMPLE YET COMPLEX
CASE STUDY

In the following section, I will present a simple case study on how we can apply the model to redesign the business of a coffee shop. I choose this example as it is easily understandable across the board, but at the same time quite complex.

This example is particularly suited as it involves several dimensions of the business: the service, the product, the image but also the management of human resources and communication. Our goal is to assess the current situation and then derive specific appropriate strategies to redesign the business of our café.

Let me introduce our case, Café Sausalito is an independent coffee shop with a unique location in the centre of the commercial district of Sham Shui Po - Hong Kong. The Founder, Michael, had emigrated to San Francisco where he studied and learned about coffee. He then decided to come back to his origins and open a coffee shop.

We will begin by analysing the current situation by grading our café business according to each principle. A deeper understanding of each business design principle will lead to the creation of entirely new strategies for our business. This strategy might be very specific or quite broad depending on the results attained in the first assessment.

For each principle, we will begin by asking five yes-or-no questions. If the answer is (YES), the score will be one (1); if the answer is (NO), the score will be zero (0). If we are uncertain or we can only partially respond to the question in our assessment, we will mark (Y/N) scoring a half point (0.5). An overall score of five (5) represents a mastery of the principle, while a score of 1 or 2 indicates a that our business is lacking in that area.

Let's begin grading our business starting from character; we will then move forward to each principle in order.

CHARACTER SCORECARD

C.I	Answer the following core statements:	Yes [1]	Y/N [0.5]	No [0]
I.1	**VALUES**: *Are our values clearly expressed and understandable?*			X
I.2	**ATTITUDE**: *Do we have a distinctive attitude and approach?*	X		
I.3	**DETAILS**: *Do we care about/own unique characterising details?*			X
I.4	**ORIGINALITY**: *Is our approach original, unconventional or disruptive?*		X	
I.5	**STRATEGY**: *Do we own a distinctive point or position? Can we maintain it over time?*			X
	Total:	1	0.5	

DESIRE SCORECARD

D.II	Answer the following core statements:	Yes [1]	Y/N [0.5]	No [0]
II.1	**BEHAVIOUR**: *Have we identified which behaviour we want to change, enhance or disrupt?*		X	
II.2	**AESTHETICS**: *Does our business/product incorporate order, harmony and clarity?*			X
II.3	**PURPOSE**: *Does our business/product serve a higher purpose besides basic function and style?*			X
II.4	**CRAFTSMANSHIP**: *Does our business/product demonstrate deep knowledge, skillfulness, technique, expertise and mastery?*			X
II.5	**IMPACT**: *Can we clearly identify which traits/features carry the most significant impact?*		X	
	Total:		1	

EMPATHY SCORECARD

E.III	Answer the following core statements:	Yes [1]	Y/N [0.5]	No [0]
III.1	**TARGET**: *Have we clearly identified a specific and unique target?*			X
III.2	**NEEDS**: *Do we have a clear vision of which needs we are providing for?*	X		
III.3	**COMMUNITY**: *Have we started a community around our business/product? Do we know who is leading and who to follow?*		X	
III.4	**STORY**: *Have we crafted a compelling, engaging and spreadable story about our business/product?*			X
III.5	**RECOGNITION**: *Have we provided our target with a symbol, a mantra and a cause?*			X
	Total:	1	0.5	

TRUST SCORECARD

T.IV	Answer the following core statements:	Yes [1]	Y/N [0.5]	No [0]
IV.1	**AUTHENTIC**: *Are we being true to our own standards and how we present ourselves?*	X		
IV.2	**COMPETENT**: *Do we have the necessary ability, knowledge, or skills to do what we promise?*	X		
IV.3	**HONEST**: *Are we acting truthfully and with sincerity; do we do what we promise we'll do?*		X	
IV.4	**RELIABLE**: *Are we consistently delivering both quality and performance while being open, connected and vulnerable?*		X	
IV.5	**FAMILIAR**: *Have we provided appropriate and crafted occasions to be often encountered or experienced?*		X	
	Total:	2	1.5	

CONSISTENCY SCORECARD

C.V	Answer the following core statements:	Yes [1]	Y/N [0.5]	No [0]
V.1	**STATUS**: *Have we crafted the overall experience surrounding our product or service? Does it grant status?*			✕
V.2	**IMAGE** vs **IDENTITY**: *Can we clearly distinguish our image from our identity?*			✕
V.3	**HUMAN CENTRED**: *Are our solutions truly human centred?*	✕		
V.4	**COLLABORATIVE**: *Is our development approach collaborative by being essential, concrete and credible?*		✕	
V.5	**EXPERIMENTAL**: *Are our processes genuinely experimental by embracing failure and identifying the next step?*		✕	
	Total:	1	1	

Now that we have the score for each principle we can start plotting the results on our spider diagram. Based on my experience, I identified that for a service-related business, the average score is 3.

	Service-related business		AVG [3.0]
I.1	CHARACTER	1.5	*Well below AVG*
I.2	DESIRE	1	*Significantly below AVG*
I.3	EMPATHY	1.5	*Well below AVG*
I.4	TRUST	3.5	*Slightly above AVG*
I.5	CONSISTENCY	2	*Below AVG*

THE MODEL - CAFÉ BUSINESS DESIGN

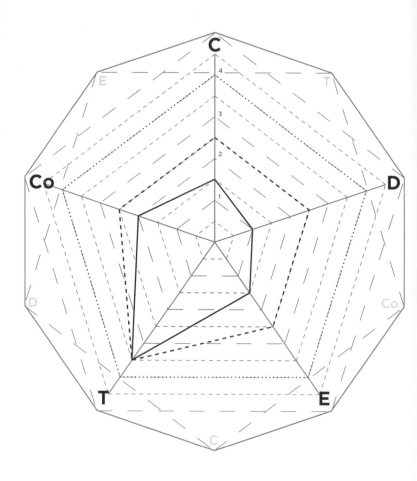

———	**As-Is Analysis**
- - - - -	Short-Term Goal
··············	Long-Term Goal

A CONTINUOUS IMPROVEMENT

Looking at our spider-gram, we can see that there is a severe imbalance within the model. As previously said, the ideal state is to keep all five principles in perfect balance, regularly monitored to guarantee a continuous improvement.

Our business design strategies must be crafted therefore with both a short-term and long-term perspective.

In the short term, we want to address the most lacking principles by raising the score as close as possible to the principle with the higher score *(trust)*, to ensure symmetry.

In the long term, we want to ensure constant growth and total harmony within the model, bringing each principle to a higher and even score.

We shall now start compiling the cheat sheets to identify areas of improvement, inspiration and meaningful insights to then craft our business design strategies.

In the following cheat sheets, I will report the answers collected by the founder of the café. Some of the answers might be incomplete or contradictory with what was previously stated and in some cases also inconclusive. Some questions have been left blank, so I compiled them on behalf of Michael. These answers are marked with an asterisk (*).

In the conclusion sections of each principle, I will present my notes and reflection on which sections have been overseen or not compiled thoroughly.

I have decided to maintain the original answers so that we could evaluate common misconceptions and avoid pitfalls when compiling your own cheat sheets.

CHARACTER CHEAT SHEET

*Whether we are creating a new design, business or brand, these simple exercises will help us lay the foundation of our first principle: **Character** (On this cheat sheet, for the sake of simplicity, "Business" will refer to any solution).*

I. VALUES: *Are our values clearly expressed and understandable?*

1. What does our business stand for?

   Connecting people through coffee

2. Describe the business in one sentence:

   Independent coffee shop from San Francisco to Hong Kong

3. Describe the business in two words; In one word

   Coffee - People   *People*

4. What is THE ONE THING our business wants to communicate/achieve?

   Building a community through coffee

II. ATTITUDE: *Do we have a distinctive attitude and approach?*

5. Business personality: What gender is our business?

   ✘ Male   Female   Both   It   None

5.1 Which age segment does our business fall into?

   Infant   Toddler   Kid   Pre-Teen   Teen

   Y-Adult   **✘** 20-30   30-40   40-50   50-60

5.2 Which socio-economic group is our business a part of?

   Low income   **✘**   High income

6. Define the following attributes of our business:

   Employment: *Barista*

   Lifestyle: *Chill - live music - Jazz musician*

   Geography: *Hong Kong - San Francisco*

7. Define our business traits *(distinguishing qualities or characteristics)*

POSITIVE	NEGATIVE
Chill	*Messy*
Talented	*Introvert (shy)*
Spontaneous	*Inconsistent*

8. Is our business…

	5	4	3	2	1	0	1	2	3	4	5	
Necessity										×		Luxury
Sweet										×		Savoury
Timeless						×						Fashionable
Amusing			×									Serious
Casual	×											Formal
Exotic								×				Familiar
Discreet			×									Aggressive
Industrial										×		Homemade
Contemporary			×									Nostalgic
Particular						×						Universal

III. DETAILS: *Do we care about/own unique characterising details?*

9. What are the nuanced details we should consider?

People, coffee, gathering, originality, connection with the area

10. What is the most pressing priority?

Generate sales	Gain awareness	× Create a community
Gain subscribers	More enquiries	Obtain information

11. What is the ONE THING that makes our business unique?

The environment, live music that connects people through coffee

12. What does success look like? Smell like? Taste like? Sound like?

All staff will be happy sharing and learn more about coffee while networking and creating a friendly environment for everyone to enjoy coffee. It will smell like strong aroma and fragrance of ground coffee. The sound of laughter interacting with each other and customers.

IV. ORIGINALITY: *Is our approach original, unconventional or disruptive?*

13. Which of the factors that the industry takes for granted should be eliminated?

> *Table service, Payment methods*

14. Which factors should be reduced well below the industry's standard?

> *Paper cups, Cash*

15. What factors should be raised well above the industry's standard?

* *Client-Barista interaction; Live music events / Attitude*

16. What factors should be created that the industry has never offered?

* *A new way of appreciating coffee*

* *A new kind of Art, Music and Creativity gathering*

V. STRATEGY: *Do we own a distinctive point or position? Can we maintain it over time?*

17. Can we state that our business is the _ _ _ in _ _ _! How?

* *Most community catalyst café in SSP*	*Fist coffee shop that offers this exp.*
* *Friendliest coffee shop in SSP*	*Friendliest staff*
* *Most creative coffee shop in SSP*	*Art and Music events*

18. Competitive substitute: *(What could replace/kill my product/service)*

> *Milk tea, Smoothies, Tea, McDonald's*
>
> *Other coffee shops, homemade coffee*
>
> *Another form of entertainment, Shopping, movies, Festivals*

19. What are the most significant available/attainable resources?

* *Specialty coffee, Competent staff, Talented artists*

* *Specialty & homemade food*

20. What are the most stringent constraints we must overcome? How?

* *Budget, human resources,*

* *Time & budget for marketing and advertising*

> *Developing a management system and people developement*

NOTES ON CHARACTER

The goal of this section, as we can identify from the scorecard, is to identify the following core elements:

VALUES:
Right off the bat, we have a very strong, powerful statement: ***"Connecting people through coffee."*** This is truly what Michael wants its business to be about. ***Chill, Talent, Spontaneous, People, Community*** are all traits that Michael associates his business with, therefore the values we can distill from this section are ***Creativity, Originality, Wellbeing, Empathy, and Care***.

ATTITUDE:
The attitude that our business is willing to convey is pretty straightforward, ***Amusing, Casual and Contemporary.***

DETAILS:
From the answers given in this section, there are few significant details that the business needs to be caring for: ***Legibility*** and ***Clarity in the message***, become more ***Tidy and Consistent***, convey a message of ***Homemade*** and ***Authenticity***.

ORIGINALITY:
At the present stage, we can't define our approach as **original**, **unconventional** or **disruptive**. The compiled answers are quite generic. We see that ***Creating a community***, ***gathering*** and ***focus on client-staff interactions*** are important factors, but how will that be achieved is not clear. In this section, we should ***describe this unique moment of interaction between staff and customer***. For example: *Imagine a taste challenge or a mini show (latte art?), a rhythm jam made with milk pitchers and mugs. We should describe any **memorable experience** we could deliver to our customers.*

STRATEGY:
How and why the values we identified as core are important, is not clear. In other words, we know we want to ***"Connect people through coffee"***, but we don't know, how and what does that truly mean. We must understand what ***actions***, ***product*** or ***service*** will make us ***connect with our target***. For example: *A secret coffee recipe, a unique menu selection, a series of significant events,* or all of the above. We are aiming to achieve a unique position where we can state: ***Sausalito is the " best " _ _ _ in town!*** Best is only one example; it could be the *cheapest, friendliest, most entertaining…*

DESIRE CHEAT SHEET

*We now have a good understanding of our values and how they shape our character. We shall proceed to identify how we make our business **desirable** for our target.*

I. BEHAVIOUR: *Have we identified which behaviour we want to change, enhance or disrupt?*

1. What problem are we trying to solve?

    Establishing connection

    What behaviour are we trying to change?

*   *Perceive coffee as a commodity drink Vs an authentic experience*

2. What needs should be fulfilled?

    Gathering — Beautiful, friendly environment

    Learn coffee — Professional development

    Good income — Status — Freedom

3. How will our business enable/empower the public?

    Be different — Be unique — Challenge the status

4. What do we want people to feel (evoke emotions)?

POSITIVE	NEGATIVE
Chill	*Social awareness*
Inspired	*Food wastage*
Refreshed/ empowered	*Conscious of bad service*

II. AESTHETICS: *Does our business/product incorporate order, symmetry, harmony, proportion and clarity?*

5. Who/What is/are our benchmarks? Why?

    Copa Vida, Equator Coffee, Café Kitsuné, Elephant Grounds

    Unique location, distinctive decor, from minimal to rustic

    Clear and distinctive offering

    Unconventional menu items

6. Describe what makes our business/product:

Useful	*Legible, iconic, recognisable, ease of application*
Usable	*Simple, Versatile, 1-2 basic colour, appetising*
Accessible	*Legibility, recognisability, distinctiveness*

7. Does our design have:

Order	*Overall identity is messy; messages are scattered*
Unity	*Identity, image and message are not aligned*
Clarity	*Our image doesn't communicates our values*
Harmony	*Communication is not always pleasing and consistent*
Proportion	*Often operations overcome image and message*

8. What kind of experience are we trying to craft?

Fun, upbeat, friendly interactions, appreciation

III. PURPOSE: *Does our business/product serve a higher purpose besides basic function and style?*

9. Besides what our design physically is, what is our design purpose?

Representing clearly our status, values and vision

10.

Who are we now?	What will we become?
Friendly	*Unique*
Approachable	*Welcoming*
Casual	*Professional*

11. How is the target acting now / solving the problem?

Starbucks, Roster, LSquare, McCafé, Common room

Bubble tea, Tea, Juice, Vending machine

12. How would they have solved the problem 50 or 100 years ago?

Homemade, Instant coffee, Town bar, Street gathering

How would they solve the problem 50 or 100 years from now?

Home machine, Coffee pills, VR

IV. CRAFTSMANSHIP: *Does our business/product demonstrate deep knowledge, skillfulness, technique, expertise and mastery?*

13. What is good about the current design? What are its physical qualities?

> *Organic, friendly, casual, warm, classy, chill, coffee colour*

14. What is bad about the actual design? (i.e. old colour schemes, outdated design...)

> *Generic look, not legible, not unified, hierarchy, inconsistent image*

15. What knowledge should the public have to fully appreciate our solution?

> *Origin / Taste / Taste notes / Owner story*

16. What skills and expertise make our business unique and inimitable?

> * *Location, Bay area look and feel, Service*

V. IMPACT: *Can we clearly identify which traits/features carry the most significant impact?*

17. What are the top 10 features of our design?

Legible	*Inspirational*
Recognisable	*Refreshing*
Unique (different)	*Sophisticated*
Professional	*Jazz*
Welcoming	*International*

18. Which 2 have the greatest impact on our business/target? How?

Recognisable	*Legible*
Screams coffee	*People can remember and spell*

19. Identify 3-5 critical touch points.

Coffee shop (signage)	*Live music events*
Kawa-open rice (app guides)	*Social Media*
Word of mouth	*Reviews and online guides*

20. What are the main PAIN POINTS we are trying to avoid?

*	*Bad coffee experience*	*Uncomfortable dining experience*
*	*Bad Service*	*No Western food in the area*

NOTES ON DESIRE

The goal of this section is to identify the following core elements:

BEHAVIOUR:
In this section, we must investigate what behaviour we want to **change**, **enhance** or **disrupt**. The current answers are a bit too generic. We must design a **life-enhancing experience**, rather than solely a service transaction. We must investigate what the real reasons to come to our cafè are. Is it gathering? Is it the food, coffee and music pairing? Is it the engagement to try to spot the new coffee? Any of these are changing the behaviour of our customer, from just grabbing a coffee, to a **unique coffee experience**.

AESTHETICS:
In this section, we can infer that there is a sense of dissatisfaction with the current brand identity. Also the **message**, **values** and **attitude** are **not well expressed**. We can see that one of the recurring themes is **inconsistency**.
This leads to the conclusion that one of the first steps to address is to restyle or rationalise Sausalito's Image and Identity.

PURPOSE:
The overall design or aesthetic of Sausalito—whether we are talking about **decor**, **identity**, **image** or any other form of communication—has the higher purpose of **connecting people**. In other words, what Michael is trying to achieve is to create an **active community**. So here we must identify what elements will drive this community to the coffee shop. To do so, we must identify what kind of aesthetics will attract and communicate to our target and why.

CRAFTSMANSHIP:
The new or refined strategy has to demonstrate **deep knowledge** and **connection to coffee** and the area. Because of its size and position, greater attention could be dedicated to delivering the **"Homemade"** or **"Creative environment"** message to the public.

IMPACT:
We should identify which traits/features carry **the most significant impact** to the desirability of the Coffee shop. I would reformulate as 1. location, 2. quality image, 3. unique decor, 4. staff personality, 5. menu items, 6. signature food, 7. atmosphere, 8. appealing Events 9. coffee quality, 10. distinctive offerings. If I had to define the greater impact, I would pick, **7. atmosphere** and **10. distinctive offerings.**

EMPATHY CHEAT SHEET

Now that we have comprehensive knowledge of the character and desire elements of our business, we shall continue by accurately analysing our target and how to empathise with them.

I. TARGET: *Have we clearly identified a specific and unique target?*

1. What's our target's gender:

   | | Male | | Female | ✗ | Both | | It | | None |

2. Which age segments is our design directed at:

   | | Infant | | Toddler | | Kid | | Pre-Teen | | Teen |

   | ✗ | Y-Adult | | 20-30 | | 30-40 | | 40-50 | | 50-60 |

3. What socio-economic group is our target a part of:

   Low income | | | ✗ | | High income

4. Define the following attributes of our target:

Employment:	*Mid-level income earners*
Lifestyle:	*DIY into spending the weekend in Sham Shui Po*
Geography:	*Expat + Kowloon resident + SSP visitors*

Now look back to the character section and determine which of our business's character traits match our target's.

II. NEEDS: *Do we have a clear vision of which needs we are, or we should be providing for?*

5. Who is our ideal customer? *(describe in detail)*

   Coffee lovers into community events and live music and DIY

6. What does he/she think & feel? *(What really matters? Worries & aspirations)*

   They all feel unique and want to makes something of themselves

7. What does he/she say & do *(Attitude, public behaviours, tone of voice, slang)*

   They are looking for fabrics or what coffee beans we have in-house

8. What are his/her pain & gains? *(fears, frustrations, obstacles/wants, achievements)*

Travelling all the way to SSP	*A great time with coffee*
Paying premium for coffee	*Great coffee + service*
Sitting in cramped space	*Get to make friends*

III. COMMUNITY: *Have we started a community around our business/ product? Do we know who is leading and who to follow?*

9. What does our target see? *(environment, friends, offers, problems)*

They see the value more than coffee been offered; they like to see how coffee is made in our presentation of the work

10. What does he/she hear? *(What do friends say? Who really influences and how?)*

They look for blogs and references. They love to discover new exciting places that others don't know about

11. Which media channels are the most influential to the target?

Facebook, Instagram, WOM, Food Apps, Trip Advisor, Yelp

12. Where can we learn about the target & his influencers?

At the Tai Nan street shops, World of coffee events

IV. STORY: *Have we crafted a compelling, engaging and spreadable story about our business/product?*

13. What is the unique story about the business he/she will spread?

A phenomenal neighbourhood coffee shop in the middle of SSP, with, warm, friendly unique designs that care about coffee and customers

14. Who will be the first follower of our target? Why? How?

DIY maker, because they strive to stand out and be unique

15. What do we know about our target?

They all look for a better quality coffee and service

Enjoy community events

There are all building their brand or family

16.   What don't we know about our target?

> *When they prefer to drink their coffee*
>
> *How they can find us*
>
> *Why do they want to come to us*

V. RECOGNITION: *Have we provided our target with a symbol, a mantra and a cause?*

17.   To which cause is our business committed to?

> *Building a community coffee shop, promote lifestyle and deliver a high-quality hospitality experience*

18.   What is the mission that we shall accomplish?

* *Create a community of creatives and entrepreneurs. Provide a space for gathering and unwinding*

19.   What is the iconic symbol that represents our Business?

* *We don't know yet!*

20.   How will our target be rewarded?

* *A unique creative environment, a strong sense of community and social gathering, knowing they are supporting an important cause to them.*

> *Loyalty program and the opportunity to become an ambassador of creativity*

Like stated before the answers marked with an asterisk (*) are the ones I compiled on behalf of our client.

NOTES ON EMPATHY

The goal of this section is to analyse our target and how to empathise with them accurately.

TARGET:

In this section, we can notice a discrepancy from the personality that we portray and the customer that we want to serve. We see that in some ways our target is **more sophisticated** than the personality we portray now.

NEEDS:

What hasn't been addressed in this section is **what makes this target unique and interesting to the coffee shop**, and what needs they have. In section 15 Michael states, **"They are all building their brand or family."** This is a unique statement, so how can we tap into this? For instance, *we could invite industry leaders and talk about specific subjects*. Understand what matters to them and link that to the coffee shop offerings. Example: *Business breakfast, sip coffee and read a business book*.

STORY:

Looking at section 13, we should be more specific about what makes Sausalito **"phenomenal"**; what makes the business **"warm friendly, unique"**; how do we exactly **"care about coffee and customers"**. If we can manage to answer these questions, we will have our unique, compelling, engaging and spreadable story about our coffee shop.

COMMUNITY:

One of the goals of this business design process is to kickstart a community around our cafè. We must identify who is leading this community and who to follow. Michael identified a few core targets: **"Coffee lovers that are into community events, and live band and DIY"** so who are these people following? Is there a super DIY celeb in HK that we can engage with? Who's the most respected coffee critic in town? Any promising young musicians we would like to support? We must be much more specific on who these people are.

RECOGNITION:

Our cause is: **"create a unique community"**. We now have to provide our target with tangible assets that will give them a reason to gather. We shall work specifically on creating a unique image and identity that goes beyond the simple brand identity. We shall look at communication materials, decor and any other form of interaction.

TRUST CHEAT SHEET

We now have a deep and relevant understanding of our target and know how to engage and communicate with them on a personal level. Now we have to demonstrate that we are worthy of their trust and affection.

I. AUTHENTIC: *Are we being true to our own standards and how we present ourselves?*

1. How does our design positively impact our target life? (min 3)

   They can relate to others when they recognise others helping;

   It would bring them memories of hanging out at Sausalito;

   It will make them wonder what coffee we have on sale;

2. What will be tangible evidence of this impact?

   More usual customers and posts on Instagram and Facebook

3. How do we maintain the integrity of our message?

   Replying to messages on Social M

   Review the videos with other managers for future improvement

   Have a YouTube channel

4. Who can we trust to maintain the integrity of our message?

   Our staff

II. COMPETENT: *Do we have the necessary ability, knowledge, or skills to do what we promise?*

5. Can we clearly restate our core promise

   * *A unique coffee experience in Sham Shui Po*

6. What skills, abilities and knowledge do we own to deliver on our promise?

   By consistently improving on our skills and hospitality

   Connect with customers, more than just a transaction

   Offering more experience of coffee

7. Can we provide tangible evidence of our operations?

   YouTube channels, coffee & workshops

8. Which skills, abilities or knowledge can we constantly improve?

_* *Customer service, cafè creations, unique menu offerings, event hosting, event planning & marketing*

III. HONEST: *Are we acting truthfully and with sincerity; do we do what we promise we'll do?*

9. What are the core promises we won't break?

Always treating customers first

More variety of coffee will be served

More workshops to connect with customers

10. Which mistakes might we make? How are we going to fix them?

Not answering questions clearly

Not planning enough for marketing

Not aligning the purpose of the event with staff

11. What are we willing to give up to maintain our promise?
(time, profit, quality, image,...)

* *Personal time, Limited offering to increase quality*

* *Investment in staff training*

* *Accept and implement feedback*

12. What is our most feared criticism? (List min. 3)

Slanders / Haters

People who would challenge just for the sake of it

Copyright issues potentially

IV. RELIABLE: *Are we consistently delivering both quality and performance while being open, connected and vulnerable?*

13. What are the minimum standards we will deliver, within which range?

Open seven days a week

Always serve coffee we are proud of

Never serve expired or spoiled products

* *Always have an open communication channel*

14. What does it take to maintain and elevate our standards?

    Having enough traffic to stay sustainable

    Sharing more knowledge and workshops

    Staying active and relevant

15. What are the tangible measures of our standards?

    How much interaction we are having with the customers

    * *Positive / negative comments on Social Media*

    * *Staff turnover and engagement rate*

16. Which industry players are setting the standards? How?

*	Starbucks	*Environment & Standards*
*	Sant'Eustachio	*Chocolate and espressos secret recipe*
	Common Room	*Art Events & Coffee*

V. FAMILIAR: *Have we provided appropriate and crafted occasions to be often encountered or experienced?*

17. With whom shall we connect to spread our message?

    Target audience, baristas around the world

18. In this moment how would our target know about our business?

    * *Strolling in Sham Shui Po, Word of Mouth, Open Rice,*

    * *Instagram, Facebook, Local food blogs*

    By attending more community and coffee events (weekly)

19. If we could buy exclusive keywords what would they be? (3-5 words)

    * *Coffee, Sham Shui Po, Live music,*

    * *Jazz, Live events, Community*

    * *San Francisco, breakfast*

20. To what extent can we open our doors to the public without compromising our intellectual property?

    Sharing recipes, coffee blend and food with one secret ingredient, getting to know the staff and people, SM profiles

NOTES ON TRUST

The goal of this section is to demonstrate to our target that we are worthy of their trust and affection. According to our scorecard, this is the highest scoring principle.

AUTHENTIC:
In this section, we can't understand what authentic offering and experience our coffee shop is providing. If for example in section 1 our statement is: a true bay area café in Hong Kong, we could state that we provide a unique *"Carnitas burrito"*, *"SF ice coffee", Imported goods from SF* or whatever is hype in SF now. If it is an authentic *crossover cafe,* we could promote *"bacon and egg sandwich",* or any old time HK favourite, *"soy milk flat white"* perhaps? The goal is presenting something that is specific and relatable.

COMPETENT:
Michael is confident that he and his team have the necessary ability, knowledge, and skills to deliver a superior coffee experience and *connect people through coffee*. Even here we must be more specific on how we can communicate that to our customers. Some ideas could be *"all our baristas have a certificate"* or *"each of them goes through 3-month apprenticeship"* or *"before becoming a Miwok* (Sausalito indigenous people) *they have to demonstrate..."*

HONEST:
This section, like the previous one, needs to be more specific on what the brand needs to achieve. *"Serve the customers within 5 minutes"* or *"have three signature events a month"* or *"Have a new blend weekly."* Also be a bit more *open to criticism* and question more the present qualities and performances.

RELIABLE:
Even this section needs to be a bit more specific. What Michael listed is true for more or less every good coffee shop on the planet. We should aim for statements such as *"listed best HK brew for two years in a row"* or *"increase SM presence with ## Weekly posts"* or *"reply to comments and criticism within 48h"* or *"implement a customer recipe every month"*.

FAMILIAR:
What exactly we have to do to be experienced. *Bring our product on the streets? Post with regularity on Social Media? How often? Be more part of local events? Which ones can we identify?*

CONSISTENCY CHEAT SHEET

Finally, we have reached the concluding stage of our development process. Now it is time to connect the dots and pull together the threads that will consolidate our Business Design.

I. STATUS: *Have we crafted the overall experience surrounding our product or service? Does it grant status?*

1. What are the intrinsic values of our product/service?

   Quality hospitality & service

   Each product is served with high satisfaction

   Never ending experiment of coffee with customers

2. What are the symbolic values of our product/service?

   Latte art

   Public demonstration of pour over

   Shop front Live Jazz

3. Which standards and behaviours do we promote and encourage?

   Volunteer for the homeless

   Avoid food wastage

   DIY handmade and trying to make something

4. Which standards and behaviours do we ban and discourage?

   Criticism

   Can't do attitudes

   Dishonest and ignorance

II. IMAGE VS IDENTITY: *Can we clearly distinguish our image from our identity?*

5. What are the traits that define our identity?

   Customer service

   Good coffee

   Live music

6. What are the traits that define our Image?

    Coffee

    S logo

    I don't know yet

7. What products/services can be confused or associated with ours?

    Nearby coffee shops with a bigger space

    Coffee shops offering more events and better service

    Other coffee shops with a sophisticated name

8. Which customs, arts, institutions do we embrace and support?

    Art Schools and Institutions in the area

    DIY Crafts

    Impact HK and other local non-profit organisations

III. HUMAN CENTRED: *Are our solutions truly human centred?*

9. What basic human needs does our business cater to?

    Interaction, Food,

    Relaxation, live music,

    Shelter, refreshment

10. Where and how is our product or service consumed?

    Instore

    Open rice

11. How can our qualities be seen, touched, smelled, tasted and heard?

    Instore

    Online

    WOM

12. What does our target know about us already?

    Western Coffee shop in Sham Shui Po

IV. COLLABORATIVE: *Is our development approach collaborative by being essential, concrete and credible?*

13. What are we going to learn in this process? From who/how?

   The right people to hire

* *Assessment of all HR and External Consultants*

   The target audience we want to focus on

* *Current customers CRM system in place*

   The core values and weaknesses of our company

* *Experimenting with different strategies and approach*

14. What unexpected skills are we going to learn/develop? From who?

   How to better stand out to customers

   Developing people and soft skills in staffs

   How to attract a potentially larger customer base

   Communication experts

   How to build a following

   Improve storytelling skills through enlightened customer exp.

15. What are the essential resources we have to rely on to succeed in our business?

   Motivated staff

   Delicious quality coffee

   More community oriented events

16. What particular method/process will become an integral part of our final outcome? How?

   Authenticity and trying to improve our latte art skills,

* *Create more workshops*

   Enlighten hospitality and inspiration connection

   Improved etiquette and constant interactions

   By creating role models

   Knowledgeable, competent staff by sending staff to competitions

V. EXPERIMENTAL: Are our processes genuinely experimental by embracing failure and identifying the next step?

17. Can we clearly identify 3 Key Performance Indicators (KPIs)

Weekly foot traffic/coffee transactions

Month-to-month growth in social media followers

Number of people we could connect with

18. What are the three areas where we absolutely won't allow any failure?

Lack of interaction with customers

Customer service

Serving bad coffee or food

19. Which mistakes might we make? How are we going to fix them?

Feeling like another similar style coffee shop they have been to

Neglecting the current trends in the market. Network with other shops and paying attention to coffee shops/ culture abroad

Not training staff properly. Implement more guidelines and making sure staff believe in our values

Sticking to our core values and competencies

20. Do we have a clear, simple and agreed-upon score to follow?

Double foot traffic every month for the next 5 years

All 4 venues combined

Be recognised as a "hidden gem in Sham Shui Po"

A tracking system in place? What does that look like?

The quantity of our events

If our foot traffic would increase over time as events increase

Staff engagement and satisfaction from improved skills through stronger revenue

NOTES ON CONSISTENCY

These simple cheat sheets do not pretend to be an ultimate guide to all things innovation, but rather a thinking trigger to put you on the right path of generating ideas and analysing problems from a different perspective. The goal of this section is to connect the dots and pull together the threads that will consolidate our Business Design.

In redesigning Sausalito's business, we must tap into **the culture** that surrounds the brand **crafting the entire experience**. We have to envision John *(young musician)* hopping into the café and start jamming with Yan playing the saxophone and enjoying coffee. How Margaret gently sips on her pour over trying to identify all of the aromas. How Tracy and Rachel are chatting at the table sharing a carrot cheese cake with a cappuccino. The goal is to **craft the overall experience surrounding our product or service**, considering variability, appropriateness, discipline and granting status.

IMAGE VS IDENTITY:
I believe one of the main reasons Michael chose to embark on a Business Design project is because he can't clearly distinguish his image from his identity. Looking back at page 101 we can recall that *"The essential duality in every brand, business or design exists between its IMAGE, a representation of its external form, and its IDENTITY, the sum of characteristics determining who or what that brand or design is"*. If we read between the lines of what Michael wants Sausalito to stand for, we can discern a pattern. He sincerely cares about **people**, **service**, **creativity** and a hint of **bohemian spirit.** Here his deep fascination with Jazz. Now the present image doesn't reflect at all the interesting desired identity. We can see in section *14. 15.* how limited his answers are.

HUMAN CENTRED:
Although he puts a lot of effort in dedicating his attention to staff and clients, he never truly describes **the real life experience that a customer can expect** by having a coffee or dining at Sausalito. Even less so on how and why a true coffee, music, DIY lover can know about and reach Sausalito.

What matters is what he/she will say about us. *"Oh, man, I went to this place, and they had the most amazing cheese sandwich ever!!!"*, or *"Went to this place, so chill and fantastic music... "*. We are the orchestrator of such conversations.
COLLABORATIVE:

Being truly collaborative means being **open** by being **essential**, **concrete** and **credible**. This doesn't translate necessarily in giving too many options, or trying to overcomplicate the offering, or simply asking customers what they want. Choice is learned not inherited.

The value of choice depends on our ability to **perceive differences between the options**. Too many choices to compare and contrast will overwhelm us. It is our duty as service providers to create a choice architecture. For instance, we could offer the 3-4 best selling coffees and then just add a *"make your own option"*. Instead of overflowing a menu with dozens of options, it should show our best offerings and eventually, add to the menu the requested customizations. For example, *if soy latte is one of the off the menu best sellers, we could add that in the new season, making it a core item.* This will show true collaboration between Customer and Service.

EXPERIMENTAL:
There is one fascinating aspect of this case study. How our client never truly **questions his business capabilities**. To embrace our business design mentality and attitude we have to embrace failure. A good designer always questions himself. I understand that this is an uncomfortable process, but we MUST question everything every time. *Is our coffee really that good? Is our food good enough? Is our staff truly as friendly as we want them to be? Are they truly willing to go the extra mile?* In all this assessment we never address this uncomfortable topic.

One of the things that I aways tell my students and clients is that as Business Designers, we should not pretend to have all the answers, but we like to think that we know how to ask the RIGHT questions.

THREE BUSINESS DESIGN STRATEGIES

This interesting case study demonstrated the foundations of my Business Design process. As we can see from our discussion, building a successful and innovative design driven business is much more that just selling (in this case) roasted beans.

We analysed and evaluated which principles our business needs to focus on to thrive in an extremely competitive market. We saw how critical it is to evaluate each principle in depth and how a simple, straightforward question can be answered in very different ways.

In this specific case of Cafè Sausalito, looking at how the difference between Image and Identity can steer the decision-making process on focussing on activities that might be very appropriate, such as a more contemporary logotype, but not necessarily essential at the present stage.

With the wealth of information gained from the cheat sheets, we were able to conceive three distinct strategies.

Strategy I   - Organisation

Strategy II   - Sophistication

Strategy III - Abstraction

These Business Design strategies should firstly lead us to bring more balance in the model by increasing the single values of Character, Desire and Empathy. Secondly, aim at a constant improvement by raising the overall value of each principle to an ideal score of 4 points.

STRATEGY I - ORGANISATION

The first strategy focuses on consolidation of the present position.

I. GOAL: Build a community of true coffee lovers that choose Sausalito as their gathering spot. Focus on recurring customer base that should account for 25-30% of revenue. Ideally, daily communication through SM with this key target, not less than weekly.

II. ENVIRONMENT: The original competitive advantage of being the first-mover in the western F&B segment is being jeopardised by new F&B establishments competing on the same sector. Newcomers have the advantage of being very specific in their offering and also enjoy the novelty factor, more modern decor and environment attracting many curious customers. To contrast this trend we shall rejuvenate the offering and image but still maintain the authenticity of the brand leveraging trust. This should lead to a tailored service for loyal customers providing solutions such as loyalty programs, personalised offerings, special payments that would make it hard for them to switch.

III. RESOURCES: We should rationalise our resources focussing on the few activities that really bear the most impact. Finance: invest on quality rather than quantity, focus the financial resources on only the most relevant items, reduce waste better to sell-out than throw-out. This should also reinforce the concept of homemade. Capitalise on HR: Be selective on staff — they truly are the ambassadors of the brand. Have dedicated staff for communication.

IV. PLAN: 1. Assess areas of improvement and define a timeline; 2. Identify the KPI's; 3. Implement a CRM system; 4. Rejuvenate the image involving key stakeholders; 5. Reassess the strategy every 3 months

V. VISION: We aim at a better understanding of the current customer base; what they like, what they need, what experience they seek. To do so, we must strengthen the line of communication and interaction between brand and target. We expect the current target to feel even more engaged with the brand. This is a quiet conservative, but methodic strategy; therefore we expect a slow but steady improvement in Character, Desire and Empathy.

STRATEGY II - SOPHISTICATION

This second strategy will focus on elevating both our offerings and our image and identity.

I. **GOAL:** Position Sausalito as the shop that delivers the true Bay Area coffee experience. We want to re-ignite the passion for coffee and gathering towards our current customer base, as well as attracting a new target customer — a more adventurous one — the type that is thrilled to discover the hidden gems. We are aiming to double foot traffic every three months for the next 3-5 years.

II. **ENVIRONMENT:** Our competitive advantage must shift from being the first-mover to being the BEST-MOVER. To do so, we must have a relentless focus on delivering great products and services at fair prices to consumers we understand intimately. We must elevate our offerings above the standard of the segment and service a targeted customer base, increasing the average spending.

III. **RESOURCES:** Even in this scenario the most important investment should be on quality, focus the financial resources on fewer most relevant items, a greater investment of time should be dedicated to elevating the quality of service and product. Focus on better sourcing of ingredients and staff. Some resource must be allocated to refresh the decor of the location and the brand collaterals. Allocate appropriate staff to the customer relationship.

IV. **PLAN:** 1. Identify what people expect from a Bay Area experience; 2. Restyle Image and identity to meet the new standard; 3. Plan for or evaluate a renovation and focus on core menu items; 4. Restructure the communication strategy to a higher standard; 5. Engage key influencers to boost popularity.

V. **VISION:** We see this strategy as slightly more daring and capital intensive, so we expect a quite higher level of engagement in the brand, boosting Character and Desirability in a relatively fast way, for Empathy and Consistency we expect a little slower adoption particularly from the newly acquired customer base.

STRATEGY III - ABSTRACTION

This strategy will focus on creating a very significant impact on the target by introducing a new service experience.

I. **GOAL:** Focus our attention on delivering a unique life experience, the atmosphere and interaction between brand and customers. Create an Identity that will be much more organic, expressive and unique. The goal is to challenge the standard offering, dedicating our attention more to coffee events and live music. Abstraction involves induction of ideas and values on a much deeper level. We want to provide at least three to four events monthly. Reach a completely new customer base that will be willing to travel to our location for our special events. We should be able to double foot traffic every 1-2 months for the next 3-5 years.

II. **ENVIRONMENT:** Our competitive advantage will be shifting from a commodity *(coffee shop)* to a Brand. We will disrupt the segment by introducing a completely new service experience focusing on environment, offerings and merchandise. We might redesign our business model more towards a subscription/brokerage fee, rather than a goods sale model.

III. **RESOURCES:** This will be the most capital intensive of all the strategies. Significant financial resources must be allocated to the creation of the new image and identity. Every detail will be redesigned towards the creation of a new brand, from interior to communication materials, any touchpoint between brand and customer. Human resources must be trained and selected to meet the new brand vision. The offering must align with the new brand direction.

IV. **PLAN:** 1. Prepare an accurate budget for the strategy; 2. Gather the necessary resources to implement the strategy; 3. Run a trial for the new business model, adjust and modify accordingly; 4. Engage key stakeholders for the launch of the new strategy; 5. Form strategic alliances between competitors and non-competitors that will reduce the time to market.

V. **VISION:** This we believe to be the most disruptive and challenging strategy of all, but as you can expect, the one that eventually, if well executed, will be the most rewarding of all three. We see a new opportunity to then expand in other locations, both nationally and internationally. The brand should be able to transcend location, product and service; delivering a new experience to customers.

CONCLUSION AND NEXT STEPS

As you can imagine, these are not the ultimate business design strategies; We created three different strategies that might be appropriate for our client's business. Another important factor to take into consideration is that these strategies are not mutually exclusive; they could be reformulated and combined to create an entirely new or a hybrid strategy.

In a way, you could also look at them as sequential strategies, from the most straightforward and less capital intensive, to the most sophisticated and more capital intensive. In their own way, each of the presented business design strategies addresses the challenges to first harmonise the model and then grow the value of each principles.

Each of the strategies will affect the principles in a different way: some might boost Character and Desire faster than Empathy and Consistency, and some others will have a milder approach, gradually increasing each principle.

For this reason, we must keep our business design model constantly monitored and evaluate each principle as we implant our business design strategy.

I will never get tired of repeating this: Business Design isn't a static process, but a dynamic one. Therefore, we must maintain a flexible mindset and be ready to react to external conditions.

I sincerely hope this simple case study was useful to help you understand how to apply the model, and can guide you in developing unique and sustainable, innovative and remarkable design businesses.

RECOMMENDED READING

Anderson, C. (2009). *Free: the future of a radical price*. New York: Hyperion.

Anderson, C. (2012). *Makers: the new industrial revolution.* New York: Crown Business.

Botton, A. D. (2004). *Status anxiety.* London: Hamish Hamilton.

Brown, T., & Kātz, B. (2009). *Change by design: how design thinking transforms organizations and inspires innovation.* New York: Harper Business.

Dixit, A. K., & Nalebuff, B. (2010). *The art of strategy: a game theorist's guide to success in business and life.* New York: Norton.

Fried, J., & Hansson, D. H. (2010). *Rework.* New York: Crown Business.

Godin, S. (2001). *Unleashing the ideavirus: stop marketing at people! turn your ideas into epidemics by helping your customers do the marketing for you.* Chicago, IL: Dearborn.

Godin, S. (2003). *Purple cow: transform your business by being remarkable.* New York: Portfolio.

Godin, S. (2012). *The Icarus deception: how high will you fly?* New York: Portfolio/Penguin.

Kelley, D., & Kelley, T. (2013). *Creative confidence: unleashing the creative potential within us all.* New York: Crown Business.

Kim, W. C., & Mauborgne, R. (2005). *Blue ocean strategy: how to create uncontested market space and make the competition irrelevant.* Boston, MA: Harvard Business School Press.

Maeda, J. (2006). *The laws of simplicity.* Cambridge, MA: MIT Press.

Martin, R. L. (2009). *The design of business: why design thinking is the next competitive advantage.* Boston, MA: Harvard Business Press.

Moore, G. A., & McKenna, R. (2000). *Crossing the chasm.* Oxford, Eng.: Capstone Pub.

Movshovitz, D. (2015). *Pixar storytelling: rules for effective storytelling based on Pixar's greatest films* North Charleston, SC: Createspace.

Osterwalder, A., Pigneur, Y., Clark, T., & Smith, A. (2010). *Business model generation: a handbook for visionaries, game changers, and challengers.* Hoboken, NJ: Wiley.

Sinek, S. (2009). *Start with why: how great leaders inspire everyone to take action.* New York: Portfolio.

Westley, F., Patton, M. Q., & Zimmerman, B. (2006). *Getting to maybe: how the world is changed.* Toronto: Random House Canada.

ACKNOWLEDGEMENTS & CREDITS

A big **thank you** to all of the people that made this book possible

Contributors in random order: Melissa Albarus, Angie Newman, Zachary Stark, Dave Leung, Yuk Man Chan, Lau Yi, Adam Newbold, Alexander de Neree tot Babberiche.

Special thanks to Michael Tam from Cafè Sausalito for letting us use his brand as a case study.

All of my wonderful colleagues and students that pushed me to finish this book.

All the kind friends and partners that had the patience to review and sustain this book.

Printed in Hong Kong

Edited by Melissa Albarus, Angie Newman, Adam Newbold

Design & Illustrations by Gianluca Cinquepalmi

First Printing, July 2017

Hard copy: ISBN 978-988-12850-0-3

PDF-ePub: ISBN 978-988-12850-1-0

www.timeless.design

Instagram: @tmlssdesign

ABOUT THE AUTHOR:

Gianluca Cinquepalmi, Associate Chair of Communication Arts and Professor of Advertising and Graphic Design at SCAD Hong Kong (Savannah College of Art and Design). In more than ten years working in the Design & Branding Industry Gianluca has managed and developed award winning agencies in Milan, Hong Kong, Barcelona and Sydney. He is now devoted to educate & train talented students, companies and institutions in the ways of attaining sustainable growth through business design.

"Most of my career has been dedicated to developing an expertise in the processes of innovation and strategical thinking; creating change-agents and teams capable of providing sustainable competitive advantage within most industries through the means of business design."